Evangelism:
A Biblical Approach

Evangelism:
A Biblical Approach

by
G. MICHAEL COCORIS

MOODY PRESS
CHICAGO

To my wife, Judy,
without whose prayers, support, and cooperation
I could never have spent thirteen years in itinerant evangelism
or have written this book

© 1984 by
THE MOODY BIBLE INSTITUTE
OF CHICAGO

The following chapters were originally printed as booklets by EvanTell, Inc., of Dallas, Texas, and are used by permission: Chapter 1, "What Is Evangelism?"; chapter 2, "Why Evangelize?"; chapter 11, "What Is Faith?" (original title: "What Is Saving Faith?"); and chapter 21, "How I Do It" (original title: "Here's How I Present the Gospel").
They have been revised.

Library of Congress Cataloging in Publication Data

Cocoris, G. Michael, 1939-
  Evangelism, a biblical approach.

  Includes bibliographical references.
  1. Evangelistic work—Biblical teaching. 2. Bible.
N.T.—Criticism, interpretation, etc. I. Title.
BS2545.E82C67   1984   269'.2   84-14681
  ISBN 0-8024-2396-5 (pbk.)

1 2 3 4 5 6 7 Printing/B + /Year 88 87 86 85 84

Printed in the United States of America

Contents

Foreword

I have a friend for whom fishing is a passion. Not only does he go after trout in Colorado, but he travels across the United States and, in fact, throughout the world to cast his line in any waters where fish are biting. When he talks about fishing, he does so with an enthusiasm and knowledge that makes me want to bait a hook myself. Aspiring anglers can learn much by spending time with such a fisherman.

Mike Cocoris has fished for men and women most of his life. I have known him for over two decades as a student, a successful evangelist, a colleague on the faculty of Dallas Seminary, and now as the pastor of a famous Los Angeles congregation. In every season of his life and in every position he has held, evengelism has been his magnificent obsession. As I have traveled across the world I have met scores of men and women whom Mike Cocoris has caught for Jesus Christ.

Like a skilled fisherman, Mike has not only thought deeply about evangelism, but he does it whenever he can. Now he has taken time from his busy schedule to share with others what he has learned through study and experience. As disciples following Jesus Christ in the world, we are summoned to go after the greatest catch of all—men and women. After reading this book, you will be motivated to throw in your line; and what is more, you will do it with greater skill.

HADDON ROBINSON

Preface

Almost from the moment of my conversion, at age 18, I wanted to be an evangelist and an expositor of the Scriptures. My involvement in both of these areas began immediately, but for the next dozen or so years a problem arose. Most of what I heard or read concerning the subject of evangelism was either a method of evangelism or a motivation to evangelize. I diligently searched for something that would expound what the Scripture has to say about evangelism. I found some helpful material here and there, and commenced my own inductive study of the Scripture. I began to formulate some conclusions.

Then I was invited to teach evangelism as an adjunct professor at Dallas Theological Seminary. For five years I lectured every fall, attempting to make the lectures as expositional and yet as practical as possible.

In 1979 I became the pastor of the Church of the Open Door in downtown Los Angeles. There I preached a series of sermons on the subject of evangelism. This book is a result of the lectures at Dallas Seminary and the sermons at the Church of the Open Door.

I am indebted to Colin McDougall, a professor at Biola University, who read and reread the manuscript and offered many helpful suggestions. My thanks also goes to Sharon Beckwith, my secretary, who typed and retyped the manuscript several times.

My prayer is that the Lord will use this material to instruct, to provoke to further study, and, above all, to motivate us to be involved in the great task of evangelism.

Part 1

The Definition of Evangelism

1

What Is Evangelism?

When you hear the word *evangelism*, what comes to mind? Many imagine a large auditorium, a crusade choir, a well-known evangelist, and a public invitation. Others think of a godly Christian quietly letting his light shine where he works. Some might even envision an over-zealous believer pistol-whipping a prospective convert with Bible verses.

Well, what is evangelism anyway?

Some claim it means changing individuals so the world will believe. Others say it means changing the world so individuals will believe. Definitions range all the way from the simple saving of souls to more complex ideas about the salvaging of society.

How does the Bible define evangelism?

If you were to search your Bible for the word *evangelize*, you would find that it is not there. In fact, the word did not appear in the English language until the seventeenth century. The problem is not that the Bible does not talk about evangelism; it obviously does. The word *evangelize* is not in most, if any, English translation of the Bible, but it is in the Greek text. So to understand what the Bible says about the subject, we must start with the Greek New Testament. There are two Greek words that must be understood before a biblical definition can be determined.

"Good News"

The first Greek word that must be understood is *euangelion*. It is a compound word, composed of *eu*, which means "good," and *angelos*, meaning "messenger." Together they form the word *euangelion*, literally meaning "good message" or "good news." The word occurs seventy-seven times in the New Testament, sixty-six of which are used by the apostle Paul.

In secular Greek *euangelion* could have been any good news. It could have been the good news that your team had won the game, or that your taxes had been reduced, or that your mother-in-law was not coming for a visit. But when this word was borrowed by the early Christians and brought into the New Testament, it was used of some specific good news, that is, the good news of Jesus Christ.

Mark introduces his gospel with "The beginning of the gospel of Jesus Christ, the Son of God." The term he uses is *euangelion*, so the verse literally means, "the beginning of the good news about Jesus Christ."

Paul is more specific. First Corinthians 15 is the only passage in the New Testament that gives a definition of the gospel.

In verses 1 and 2, Paul says he is about to declare to them the gospel by which they were saved. Then, in verses 3 to 5 he defines that gospel. These verses say four things about Christ: He died for our sins; He was buried; He arose; and He was seen. Notice that twice Paul adds the phrase "according to the Scriptures," indicating that the two basic elements of the gospel are: Christ died for our sins; and Christ arose from the dead. Why then did he add that Christ was buried and was seen? The answer is that His burial is proof of His death, and His appearances are proof of His resurrection. Whatever else evangelism is, it has to do with the death and resurrection of Christ.

"Announce the Good News"

The second Greek word that must be understood is *euangelizō*, translated "evangelize." It means "to announce the good news"— any good news. To announce to an anxious student that he has earned an A on an exam; to announce to a fearful patient that the diagnosis was not cancer; to announce to a nervous expectant father that he has a healthy baby; all these are ways of "evangelizing."

euangelizō is used fifty-five times in the New Testament. This verb is used in a general way. In 1 Thessalonians 3:6, Paul says, "But now that Timothy has come to us from you, and brought us good news of your faith and love..." The phrase "brought us good news" is the verb *euangelizō.* Timothy announced to Paul the good news of their spiritual health. This is the term *evangelize* in its general sense.

However, in the New Testament *euangelizō* is usually translated "preach the gospel." It refers specifically to the gospel of Jesus Christ. Paul says in 1 Corinthians 1:17, "For Christ did not send me to baptize, but to preach the gospel," literally, "... not to baptize, but to evangelize." In 1 Corinthians 9:16 he says, "Woe is me if I do not preach the gospel!" In these and many other passages, Paul is using *euangelizō,* meaning "to announce the good news of Jesus Christ." So to evangelize in the New Testament sense of the term is to announce the good news that Jesus Christ died for our sins and arose from the dead.

The phrase "preach the gospel" is usually the translation of the Greek verb *euangelizō.* However, it is sometimes the translation of the Greek word for "preach," *kerusso,* combined with the Greek word for "gospel" (*euangelion*). C. H. Dodd says,

> The verb "to preach" frequently has for its object "the gospel." Indeed the connection of ideas is so close that "preach" by itself can be used as a virtual equivalent for "to evangelize," or "preach the gospel." It would not be too much to say that whenever preaching is spoken of it always carries with it the implication of good tidings proclaimed.[1]

When Paul says in 1 Corinthians 1:17, "For Christ did not send me to baptize, but to preach the gospel," the Greek text for "preach the gospel" is simply *euangelizō,* "to evangelize." But in Mark 16:15 when the Lord says, "Go into all the world and preach the gospel to every creature," the text contains *kērussō,* the verb "to preach," and the noun *euangelion,* "the gospel." They are simply two different ways of saying the same thing.

EVANGELISM IS...

Having looked at the meaning of these two Greek words, have

---

1.   C. H. Dodd, *The Apostolic Preaching and Its Development,* p. 8.

we arrived at a definition of evangelism? Is evangelism announcing the good news that Jesus Christ died for our sins and arose from the dead?

Just determining the meaning of a word does not fix the definition. Theological definitions are often determined by the meaning of words and the *use* of those words in the Bible. For example, the word for "church" (*ekklēsia*) means "called out ones; assembly." But the way that word is *used* in the New Testament indicates that an *ekklēsia* is an organized group of baptized believers.

Is evangelism just announcing the good news of Christ, or does the use of that word in the New Testament demand more? Obviously, something needs to be added. Would it be evangelism if a pastor just announced the gospel to a group of believers? A skeptic could also announce the gospel, attempting to discredit it. So merely announcing the good news of Jesus Christ is certainly not evangelism. What, then, must be included? I propose the following:

 Evangelism is communicating the gospel of Jesus Christ with the immediate intent of converting the hearer to faith in Christ, and with the ultimate intent of instructing the convert in the Word of God so that he can become a mature believer.

In the New Testament, Christians did not just present the truth about Christ; they presented truth about Christ in order to secure a decision for Christ. True, they began with a proclamation of facts about Him, but the facts led to an appeal. In Acts 14:15 Paul says, "We...preach to you that [in the Greek this is a clause denoting purpose] you should turn from these vain things to the living God." In Matthew 4:19 Jesus tells the disciples He will make them fishers of men. There is a purpose, or at least an intent, in fishing: to catch fish. The immediate purpose or intent in announcing the gospel is that people will trust Christ.

Yet the New Testament does not stop there. The Great Commission means more than making Christians; it means making disciples. In Colossians 1:28 Paul says, "Him we preach, warning every man and teaching every man in all wisdom, that we may present every man perfect in Christ Jesus." The ultimate goal in the New Testament is to instruct believers in the Word of God so that they may become mature. This maturity includes personal spiritual growth and service in the context of a local church.

My definition of evangelism consists of two elements: information and intent. Practically, this amounts to informing people about Christ (especially His death for sin and His resurrection) and inviting them to trust Him. Information without invitation may be instruction, but it is not evangelism. Likewise, invitation without instruction may be exhortation, but not evangelism. This does not mean that every time there is information there must be an invitation. It may be that in a given situation wisdom dictates that there be information without invitation. That has a place—it is called pre-evangelism. But evangelism proper is the communication of the gospel with a view to conversion.

In his book *Evangelism and the Sovereignty of God* J. I. Packer says, "How then should evangelism be defined? The New Testament answer is very simple. According to the New Testament, evangelism is just preaching the gospel, the evangel." He then adds, "Evangelizing, therefore, is not simply a matter of teaching, and instructing, and imparting information to the mind. There is more to it than that. Evangelism includes the endeavor to elicit a response to the truth taught. It is communication with a view to conversion. It is a matter, not merely of informing, but also of inviting."[2]

In defining evangelism some have missed the New Testament concept altogether. Liberals have defined it as social action. They speak of "presence evangelism," which means to become involved in what God is doing in the world—to campaign against all that dehumanizes man. Presence could be anonymous and silent; the name of Christ could or could not be mentioned. This statement goes on to define evangelism as "redeeming social structures" and "reconciling hostile men and nations." Harvey Cox has been quoted as saying, "Any distinction between social action and evangelism is mistaken."[3]

Against this backdrop Billy Graham has said,

> I maintain that evangelism is much more than non-verbal witness. Humanists may heal, feed, and help, but social presence isn't Gospel presentation. The Gospel is an announcement of the Good News. But what Good News? It is the thrilling proclamation that Jesus Christ, the very God and very man, died for my sins on the cross, was buried, and arose the third day. The Son has made full atonement for my sins. If I reach forth by faith to receive Christ as my personal Savior, I am declared forgiven by God, not through any merit of mine but

2. J. I. Packer, *Evangelism and the Sovereignty of God,* pp. 41, 50.
3. C. Peter Wagner, "What Is Evangelism?" pp. 96-7.

through the merit of Christ's shed blood. . . . Biblically, evangelism can mean nothing else than proclaiming Jesus Christ by presence, by word, and by trusting the Holy Spirit to use the Scriptures to persuade men to become His disciples and responsible members of His church.[4]

In defining evangelism some do not go far enough, and others go too far. For example, some would suggest that evangelism is simply proclamation. According to them, Christians are to proclaim the gospel—period. That is not going far enough. We must inform and invite. Others go to the other extreme. They would say that evangelism is persuasion. According to this viewpoint, Christians are to lead people to Christ, but it is not evangelism until people get saved. That is going too far; God gives the increase. First Corinthians 3:6 says, "I planted, Apollos watered, but God gave the increase." We must inform and invite. Skill in evangelism depends on us. Success in reaping depends upon God.

Telling someone about your conversion is not evangelism; nor is telling someone about your creed, although those techniques may be helpful in getting attention or creating a sense of need. Convincing someone to walk down an aisle or to sign a card is not necessarily evangelism. Evangelism is communicating the gospel and inviting the person to trust Christ.

What is a marriage proposal? If all a fellow did was give his girl information, such as "I love you," she would wonder when, or even if, he was going to pop the question. On the other hand, if he just grabbed her hand and marched up to the justice of the peace without any previous discussion, most girls would object; that's going too far too fast. A proposal means communicating your love to your sweetheart and inviting her to be your wife. It is information and invitation. Likewise, evangelism is communicating the gospel with the intent of converting the person to faith in Jesus Christ.

Since the ultimate purpose of the New Testament is to make us mature in Christ, evangelism must be immediately followed by instruction. But that is the result of evangelism, and not evangelism itself. The Lausanne Covenant says it well: "But evangelism itself is the proclamation of the historical, biblical Christ as Saviour and Lord, with a view of persuading people to come to Him personally

4. Billy Graham, "Why Lausanne?" p. 8.

and so be reconciled to God. . . . The results of evangelism include obedience to Christ, incorporation into His church and responsible service in the world."[5]

5.   "Lausanne Covenant," pp. 22–23.

Part 2

The Biblical Bases of Evangelism

2

Why Evangelize?

Why evangelize?
  Why even ask the question?

For a Christian to question evangelism is like an American questioning apple pie, the stars and stripes, and motherhood. Yet the question needs to be asked, and answered. For those Christians who are already involved in evangelism, the question needs to be answered so that the right thing will be done for the right reason. For believers not involved in evangelism, the question needs to be answered so that the right thing will be done.

What, then, is the basis of evangelism?

To answer that, I will consider five passages of Scripture in the next five chapters. The first is Matthew 28:16–20:

> Then the eleven disciples went away into Galilee, to the mountain which Jesus had appointed for them. And when they saw Him, they worshiped Him; but some doubted. Then Jesus came and spoke to them, saying, "All authority has been given to Me in heaven and on earth. Go therefore and make disciples of all the nations, baptizing them in the name of the Father and of the Son and of the Holy Spirit, teaching them to observe all things that I have commanded you; and lo, I am with you always, even to the end of the age." Amen.

This incident took place on the mountain in Galilee, and several groups were present.

First, the disciples were there. Verse 16 says, "Then the eleven disciples went away into Galilee."

Second, it is likely that over five hundred were there. Paul told the Corinthians in 1 Corinthians 15:6 that Christ "was seen by over five hundred brethren at once." None of the gospel accounts say when that took place, but one clue may help solve the problem. Of the ten post-resurrection appearances of Christ, only one, the one recorded in this paragraph, was preannounced and thus prearranged. Notice that verse 16 says, "To the mountain which Jesus had appointed for them." Since this is the only time Christ announced ahead of time when and where He would appear, students and scholars have concluded that this is the time when five hundred plus saw Him.[1]

Third, you were there. Verse 20 says, "Lo, I am with you always, even to the end of the age." What Christ had to say on this occasion He meant to apply to all believers until the end of the age. So at least in His mind, you were there.

On this occasion, the Lord gave the complete Great Commission to those present. A careful study of it is required.

THE AUTHORITY FOR THE GREAT COMMISSION

Christ asserts in verse 18, "All authority has been given to Me." There are two different Greek words sometimes translated "power." *dunamis* means the ability to perform and is properly translated "power." *exousia* means the right to use power and is properly translated "authority." Christ uses the second word. He is claiming He has all authority, that is, the ability to do all things and the right to use that ability.

To illustrate the difference between power and authority, suppose I walked out of a bank and for no reason at all, a 250-pound, six-foot-four-inch madman came charging down the street, flew into me, and sprawled me all over the sidewalk. He, being bigger than I, has power; but he has no right to do that. On the other hand, suppose I had just robbed that bank, and it was a

---

1. That would explain the difficulty in verse 17, where it says that they worshiped Him, but some doubted. How could people worship and doubt at the same time? Perhaps that is possible, but more likely the ones who worshiped were the disciples, and the doubters were among the five hundred. (See for example Alfred Plummer, *An Exegetical Commentary on the Gospel According to S. Matthew*, p. 427.)

250-pound, six-foot-four-inch policeman who tackled me. He would have authority—the ability and the right to use that ability. That is what Christ is claiming. He has all authority in all the universe.

He claims all authority in heaven. Why does He say that? Paul gives us the answer in Ephesians 6:12. The real spiritual battle is in the heavenlies: "For we do not wrestle against flesh and blood, but against principalities, against powers, against the rulers of the darkness of this age, against spiritual hosts of wickedness in the heavenly places." Those evil powers (*exousia,* literally "authorities," the same Greek word as in Matt. 28:18) wage war against believers, especially those who are involved in carrying out the Great Commission. Christians wrestle against authorities, but Christ has all authority, even in the heavenlies.

If a Christian is to be successful in carrying out the Great Commission, he must be aware of, and appeal to, the authority of Christ.

I have often sensed satanic opposition to evangelism. During one united crusade, everything started going wrong. The sponsoring committee and the participating pastors were at odds. There was bickering and backbiting. The people came, but the blessing of God was absent. After several days of defeat I called the evangelistic team together and suggested that the problem was satanic. We prayed earnestly, pleading Christ's authority over evil powers. It was then that we were drenched with the blessing of God. Attitudes changed, relationships mended, and sinners were converted.

Christ not only claims all authority in heaven, but He also claims to have all authority on earth. When Christ walked on the earth, He exercised authority over nature (e.g., the stormy sea). If a Christian is to be successful in fulfilling the Great Commission, he must be aware of, and appeal to, the authority of Christ.

His earthly authority is not only over nature but over nations. Daniel 4:25 tells us, "The Most High rules in the kingdom of men." More than one missionary, being hindered in God's work, has appealed to that higher court and has demonstrated that God is greater than government. Some have lost the appeal, and their lives: they are called martyrs. The point is that God has all authority, and He sovereignly chooses when to use it.

THE TASK OF THE COMMISSION — TO MAKE DISCIPLES

Based on His claim ("therefore"), He issues a command. The

King James Version says, "Go ye therefore, and teach all nations" (v. 19), causing a misunderstanding: it sounds as though there are two commands, "to go" and "to teach." The Greek text, however, has only one command: "to make disciples." Making disciples (*mathēteuō*) is the only imperative in this paragraph. Clustered around that imperative are three participles: "going," "baptizing," and "teaching." The main verb ("make disciples") tells what is to be done, and the participles ("going," "baptizing," "teaching") tell how it is to be done. So the command is to make disciples.

Some contend that "disciple" is a synonym for "Christian." In that view, to make a disciple is to make a Christian. But this and other biblical passages indicate that being a Christian is one thing and being a disciple is another. Being a Christian costs nothing; salvation is a gift. Discipleship costs everything (Luke 14:25–35). Thus, a disciple is defined as a baptized believer who is obeying the word and is therefore growing in the Lord.

The three participles indicate the three-step process in disciple-making. Step one is "going." This participle (*poreuthentes*) could be translated "as you go" or "having gone." The Lord does not amplify on the going here. But in Mark 16:15–16 He adds, "Go [the same Greek word and construction as in Matt. 28:19] into all the world and preach the gospel to every creature. He who believes and is baptized will be saved; but he who does not believe will be condemned." Evidently, betweeen the going and baptizing comes presenting the gospel and inviting the person to Christ.

Step two is "baptizing" (*baptizontes*). The New Testament teaches that when a person hears the message about Jesus Christ and trusts Him as Savior, he has eternal life (John 3:36). Then he is to be baptized. Luke indicates that order throughout Acts. That is always the order: hear, believe, and be baptized (e.g., Acts 18:8). Peter says that baptism is a symbol (1 Pet. 3:18). Just as a wedding ring is a symbol of the union between a man and a woman, so baptism is a symbol of a believer's union with Jesus Christ (Rom. 6:3–5). Baptism also identifies a believer with a body of believers. The Lord indicates that baptism is to be done in the name of the Father, and of the Son, and of the Holy Spirit.[2]

Step three is "teaching" (*didaskontes*). When a person has trusted

---

2. Paul says "in the name" and then gives three names. Grammatically that is incorrect, but theologically it is precise. There is one God who exists in three persons.

Christ as Savior and has been baptized, he is to be taught. Verse 20 says he is to be taught "all things that I have commanded you." Secular teaching today, especially in university classrooms, is nothing more than content for the mind. Teaching in the church must be more. It must include commands for the will.

Thus, the threefold process of disciple-making is to (1) introduce a person to Christ, (2) identify him with the Body of Christ, and (3) instruct him in the commands of Christ.

THE EXTENT OF THE COMMISSION

Matthew 28:19 says to disciple all nations. Earlier in the gospel of Matthew, Christ has sent the disciples to the lost sheep of the house of Israel (Matt. 10:5-6). Now He sends them to all nations. That is one of the reasons this is called the Great Commission. The extent of the Great Commission is global.

THE POWER FOR THE COMMISSION — THE SPIRITUAL PRESENCE OF CHRIST

In verse 20 Christ says, "Lo, I am with you always, *even* to the end of the age." In Greek the "I" is emphatic (*egō*). The "I," of course, is Jesus Christ. He may be identified as the Son of God or as the Savior of men, but in this paragraph He has identified Himself as the One who has all authority in heaven and earth (v. 18). So when He says "I" emphatically in verse 20, He is reminding them that the One who has all authority in heaven and on earth will be with them.

Furthermore, Christ will be spiritually present with the disciple-makers always, in season and out of season, in sunshine and in shadows. He will be with them in peacetime and in persecution, in success and in failure, now and until He returns.

The goal of the church, then, is to make disciples. That includes *both* evangelism and edification. Some preach as if the goal is only evangelism. Others teach that the goal of the church is edification. In their view the church is a school, not a soul-saving station. But it is not either/or; it is both/and. The goal is to make disciples.

Christ is saying to His disciples in the first century, and to all disciples in every century until He returns, "As the One who has all authority, I command you to make disciples of all nations, and I will personally be with you as you go." In other words, with the goal of Christ before, the presence of Christ beside, and the authority of Christ behind, disciples are to march into all the world and make disciples.

3

The Confirmation

Matthew 28:18–20 is commonly called the Great Commission. Actually, there are five passages in the New Testament that record the Great Commission. To fully understand that great charge to the church, all five must be studied in detail.

Our second passage is Mark 16:14–18:

> Afterward He appeared to the eleven as they sat at the table; and He rebuked their unbelief and hardness of heart, because they did not believe those who had seen Him after He had risen. And He said to them, "Go into all the world and preach the gospel to every creature. He who believes and is baptized will be saved; but he who does not believe will be condemned. And these signs will follow those who believe: In My name they will cast out demons; they will speak with new tongues; they will take up serpents; and if they drink anything deadly, it will by no means hurt them; they will lay hands on the sick, and they will recover."[1]

[handwritten margin note: Contradicts prior statement about Baptism]

1. Doubt has been cast on the genuineness of this passage, but the evidence argues for its inclusion in the text. It occurs in the vast majority of Greek manuscripts. As a matter of fact, it is in every Greek manuscript of Mark except two; and in one of the two, there is a blank space left for it. These verses are included in many of the ancient versions, including the Vulgate and the Syriac, which date from the second century, and the Coptic, which goes all the way back to AD 150. It was alluded to in AD 151 by Justin, and quoted by Titian, Justin's disciple. Critics of the passage quote Jerome to defend their view, but Jerome included it in the Vulgate. A detailed defense of the authenticity of these verses is presented in John Bergon, *The Last Twelve Verses of Mark*.

In this passage Jesus focuses on the evangelistic command and the confirmation of the commission to the first-century disciples. The disciples here were not on a mountain in Galilee waiting for the Lord to appear; rather, they were sitting in a room (probably in Jerusalem) eating. Verse 14 informs us that at this point the disciples refused to believe the resurrection. That is remarkable! Mark 8 records that the Lord had told them He was going to die and be raised. After the crucifixion He sent them three announcements that He was alive (cf. carefully Mark 16:7, 11, 13). Yet after all of that, they still did not believe. Their unbelief can be traced throughout this chapter (vv. 13–14). The turn of events had plunged them into disbelief, disobedience, and probably despondency.

Their unbelief affected them radically. Verse 14 says the Lord "rebuked their unbelief and hardness of heart." The unbelief produced the hardness. The word "heart" here (*kardia*) probably refers to the whole inside of the person, his intellect, emotions, and will. Inside they were hard. One commentator says this refers to the "inaction of the whole heart, in its widest sense, including intellect as well as feeling."[2] They were shocked, stunned, almost stupefied—their unbelief had paralyzed them. In the midst of their spiritual malady, the Lord manifested Himself. Jesus "rebuked" them. The word (*oneidizō*) means to reproach, to blame, to censor. He chided them. They should have believed and did not. So the Lord sternly rebuked them to arouse them out of their disbelief and discouragement.

Fascinating, isn't it? We would think that a command of this scope and consequence would be given to those who were able to accomplish the task: to political, military, or religious leaders; or perhaps to a company of intellectual giants who by sheer force of genius might accomplish it. Instead, the Lord gave the Great Commission to a small group of obscure Galileans whose names had never been uttered in the Roman senate. Caesar had never heard of them, and they were frozen in unbelief.

THE TASK OF THE COMMISSION – TO PREACH THE GOSPEL

After the Lord chided them, He commanded them to go into

---

2. J. A. Alexander, *Commentary on the Gospel of Mark*, p. 441.

all the world and preach the gospel to every creature. The Greek text literally says, "Going, preach the gospel." The command is not to go, but to preach—the going is assumed.

Mark titles his book "The gospel [good news] of Jesus Christ" (Mark 1:1). In 1:14, he talks about the good news of the coming of the Kingdom. In 8:31, he tells us that Jesus informed His disciples that He would die and rise again. Toward the end of Mark's gospel, the word "gospel" (*euangelion*) is used to refer to Christ's death (14:9). After the resurrection, and probably after the incident in this passage, Christ gave His disciples a discourse on His death and resurrection. It is not until later, however, that Paul defines the gospel as the death and resurrection of Christ (1 Cor. 15).

A long line of martyrs have died rather than deny what they believed. Unlike Stephen, Christ did not die as a mere martyr. Nor did Christ die just to exhibit the love He had for the world. Nor even did He die to convince men that He loved them. He died as a substitute. A. B. Simpson is reported to have said that the gospel "tells rebellious men that God is reconciled, that justice is satisfied, that sin has been atoned for, that the judgment of the guilty may be revoked, the condemnation of the sinner cancelled, the curse of the Law blotted out, the gates of hell closed, the portals of heaven opened wide, the power of sin subdued, the guilty conscience healed, the broken heart comforted, the sorrow and misery of the Fall undone."

The command is to preach the gospel, but that is not the complete task. Verse 16 says, "He who believes and is baptized will be saved." Thus, when people believe, they are to be baptized. This is not saying, however, that one must be baptized in order to be saved. The verse does not say, "Be baptized in order to be saved," it says, "He who believes and is baptized." It is like saying that if you get on the bus and sit down, you will go to New York. Technically, if you just get on the bus you will make it to New York. Being baptized does not save. Omitting baptism does not condemn. Matthew's account goes beyond baptism to include teaching them after they are baptized. The result of all this is the establishment of a local church.

THE EXTENT OF THE COMMISSION

This great and glorious good news is to be preached in all the world. Did the disciples obey? Did they go into all the world, or did they stay in Jerusalem? In Colossians 1:16, Paul says the gospel did go into all the world. Whether or not Paul means that they preached in every nation of the world, no one knows. But tradition records that the disciples did not stay in Palestine.

Various traditions have reported the following movements of the disciples. Peter went to Babylon and Rome, where he was crucified upside down. Supposedly his bones have been discovered there. Andrew reportedly went to southern Russia and ended up in Ephesus in Asia minor, that is, modern Turkey. James, the son of Zebedee, probably went to Spain between Acts 2 and Acts 12. Acts 12 records that he was killed in Jerusalem by Herod Agrippa. John went to Ephesus and probably elsewhere. One tradition is that Philip went to France. Bartholomew, identified as Nathaniel, is said to have gone to Asia minor, and then eastward to Armenia (an area divided today between Iran and the Soviet Union), where he was skinned alive before he was beheaded. Tradition also says that Thomas preached in Persia, where he met the three wise men, whom he baptized. He then is supposed to have taken them with him to India. Matthew stayed in the Holy Land for fifteen years and then supposedly went to Persia and Ethiopia, where he met Philip. James, the son of Alpheus, went to Syria. Jude went to Armenia, Syria, and northern Persia. Simon the Canaanite traveled to Egypt, then to Carthage, to Spain, and then to Britain, where he met Joseph of Arimathea. Then he journeyed to Syria, Mesopotamia, and was martyred in Persia.

However, the command is to preach the gospel not only in all the world, but to every creature. Nowhere has the gospel been given to every creature. The gospel has been preached for centuries in the United States. There are many churches with thousands in them, and many more with hundreds. This is the evangelical center of the world. Yet there are hundreds, thousands, and probably millions of individuals who have never heard or understood the gospel. And the Lord does not mean for one to be left out.

CONFIRMATION OF THE COMMISSION – SIGNS

Christ promised His unbelieving disciples that signs would follow those who believed. These were confirming signs: Mark 16:20 says that they were to confirm the Word, and Paul indicates that these types of miracles confirm the apostolic office (2 Cor. 12:12). Both the message and the messenger were to be confirmed by signs.

The book of Acts records that four of the five kinds of signs occurred. Peter, Philip, and Paul cast out demons. Tongue speaking occurred. Paul did not "take up" a serpent; but one "took up" with him, and he lived to tell about it. Peter and Paul healed the sick. There is nothing in Acts to indicate that anyone drank any poison, but church history contains a well-known story concerning the apostle John: a fatal potion was prepared for him, but when he drank it, he was unhurt.

Do these signs confirm the message today? There is evidence that confirming signs have ceased. Hebrews 2:3–4 does not say the message was confirmed directly by signs, but was "confirmed to us by those who had heard." In other words, one group got the signs, the next generation did not. The second group was not confirmed by signs but by the group who got the signs.

4

The Message

Then He said to them, "These are the words which I spoke to you while I was still with you, that all things must be fulfilled which were written in the Law of Moses and the Prophets and the Psalms concerning Me." And He opened their understanding, that they might comprehend the Scriptures. Then He said to them, "Thus it is written, and thus it was necessary for the Christ to suffer and to rise from the dead the third day, and that repentance and remission of sins should be preached in His name to all nations, beginning at Jerusalem. And you are witnesses of these things. Behold, I send the Promise of My Father upon you; but tarry in the city of Jerusalem until you are endued with power from on high." [Luke 24:44–49]

In Luke's account, it appears that everything after the resurrection happened on the day of the resurrection. But that cannot be. In Luke 24, the disciples are told to tarry in Jerusalem; but in Matthew 28, they are told to meet on a mountain in Galilee. Therefore, during the time span of Luke 24, there must have been a trip to Galilee. These observations have driven commentators to the conclusion that Luke 24 is Luke's summary of all that was said after the resurrection. Others believe that it is a summary of what Christ said on the Mount of Olives.

THE MESSAGE OF THE COMMISSION —THE GOSPEL

Jesus began by reminding them that He had taught them the

Scriptures. Luke records such incidents for us in Luke 9:22; 18:31-33; 17:25; and 22:37. The Law, the Prophets, and the Psalms were the ancient Jewish divisions of the Old Testament. Thus, Christ is saying that every major part of the Old Testament speaks of Him and must be fulfilled. (The Old Testament Christ refers to here is identical to the Old Testament today. The divisions are different, but the content is exactly the same.)

He told them that they did not understand. Often one does not learn something the first time he hears it. So He opened "their understanding, that they might comprehend the Scriptures" (v. 45). Spiritual things can only be discerned spiritually. What they had heard, but had not understood, was the gospel.

Christ told them it was written that He should suffer and be raised from the dead the third day. But it is possible to hear and not hear, to see and not see. That is especially true of the gospel. Satan blinds the minds of those that do not believe. Only God can make them see.

After Jesus explained the Scriptures, He exhorted them to preach repentance and remission of sins. Mark 16 indicates that when a person hears the gospel, what he needs to do is believe. But in this passage the Lord says repentance is to be preached. Evidently, biblical faith assumes repentance, and biblical repentance includes faith (we will deal with this further in chapter 10).

They were also to preach the remission of sins, that is, forgiveness. This was to be done "in His name" (literally translated, "*on* His name"), indicating that the name of Christ is to be the ground upon which the offer of forgiveness is made. The epistles explain further that forgiveness is based on the cross of Christ (e.g., Col. 1:14). Actually, the Luke 24 passage implies that. In verses 44-46 Christ says that the Old Testament prophesied His death and resurrection. He predicted it; He performed it; now He says, "Go preach it." The implication is that His death and resurrection form the basis for forgiveness.

This is an important issue. The basis for forgiveness is not that God likes us or even that He loves us. It is that Christ laid down His life for us to pay for our sins. Some think forgiveness is like a man's saying to the child down the block who threw a ball through his window, "It's OK, kid. I like you. Forget it." No, God is love, but He is also righteous and just. Forgiveness is like a child's throwing a

1. John R. Stott, "The Great Commission," p.55.

ball through a window, and the owner's son paying for the broken glass. Then the man says, "It's all right; my son paid for it." G. Campbell Morgan once said, "If God would forgive me without the cross, then I would never be satisfied with His forgiveness."

THE EXTENT OF THE COMMISSION

Preaching is to be done among all nations, beginning at Jerusalem. Earlier, Christ had sent the disciples out, but only to Israel. Now He sends them to the Gentiles. He sent them to one nation; now He sends them to all nations. Jesus was no mere teacher who founded a Jewish sect. The gospel of Luke presents Him as the Son of Man, who comes to be the Savior of all who trust in Him. John R. Stott says concerning this passage, "The church, in other words, is fundamentally a missionary society, commissioned and committed to proclaim the Gospel of salvation to the whole world."[1]

This preaching to the whole world was to begin at Jerusalem. For the disciples, Jerusalem was not home, Galilee was home. Jerusalem was where they were at the moment. The principle: evangelism begins where you are.

THE POWER OF THE COMMISSION

Jesus told them that they were to be witnesses (the apostles were eyewitnesses of the death and resurrection of Christ); then He told them that He would send "the Promise of the Father." What is that? Acts 1:4 uses that phrase and adds, ". . . which you have heard from Me." "The Promise," then, refers to the promise Christ gave in the Upper Room discourse concerning the coming of the Holy Spirit (John 14:16-26; 16:7-15).

He also told them to tarry in Jerusalem because the coming of the Holy Spirit was to be on the day of the Feast of Pentecost. So they had to wait, not to convince God to give them the Holy Spirit, but so the day of the annual Feast of Pentecost could arrive and God's program could be fulfilled.

He called this coming of the Holy Spirit being "endued with power." The Greek word *enduō* literally means "clothed" and is used in Ephesians 4:24, Colossians 3:10-12, Romans 13:14, and Galatians 3:27. If you have trusted Christ, you have been endued just like the apostles.

So Christ's command in Luke is: Once you understand the Scripture and have received the Holy Spirit, then preach repentance and remission of sins among all nations. The Lord chose to emphasize the message of the Great Commission.

The charge of the church is not to heal the sick. Christ had earlier charged the twelve, and also the seventy, to heal the sick (Luke 9:12; 10:9). That charge is absent here. God can, and does, supernaturally heal the sick, but miraculous healing (the instantaneous and complete healing without the use of medical means) is not part of Christ's commission to the church. The church today has no authority to exercise a regular ministry of miraculous healing. The primary task of the church is heralding the gospel.

Christians ought to be the salt of the earth and the light of the world. They should influence society and illuminate its darkness. They must be responsible citizens and even provoke reform on occasions. But the primary task of church members is to herald the gospel, not reform society.

5

The Power

Then, the same day at evening, being the first day of the week, when the doors were shut where the disciples were assembled, for fear of the Jews, Jesus came and stood in the midst, and said unto them, "Peace be with you." Now when He had said this, He showed them His hands and His side. Then the disciples were glad when they saw the Lord. Then Jesus said to them again, "Peace to you! As the Father has sent Me, I also send you." And when He had said this, He breathed on them, and said to them, "Receive the Holy Spirit. If you forgive the sins of any, they are forgiven them; if you retain the sins of any, they are retained." [John 20:19-23]

The disciples were plagued by fear. The evening of resurrection day found them shut up in a room for fear of the Jews. On one of the greatest days in the history of the world, when men should have been dancing in the street, they were trembling in their locked room.

Of course, they had a reason to be afraid. The Jews had just managed to see to it that Jesus was put to death. The disciples were His closest companions and His designated disciples. Now that Christ was removed, perhaps the bitter hatred of the Jews would be focused on the apostles.

In their isolation and dread, Jesus appeared suddenly, supernaturally. Verse 19 says the door was securely shut. That must have frightened them. But with His presence, Christ brought peace. The solution for fear is the presence of Christ, which brings peace. In Matthew 28:20, He promises to be with us always, even to the end of the age. In Philippians 4:6-7, Paul assures us that as we pray, His peace will guard our hearts and minds. So Christ calmed them with His presence and with His peace. He does the same for believers today.

Fear was not their only problem. Verse 20 implies that they were also perplexed by doubt. What is here implied is clearly stated in Mark 16:14. We wonder how they could possibly doubt the Lord. After all, the Old Testament had prophesied the resurrection, and Jesus Himself had proclaimed it to them. On top of that, Mary had seen Him, and so had Peter. How could they doubt?

One possible answer is that they were looking for Christ to establish a literal kingdom. Though He had told them He was about to die, they were so convinced that He was about to bring in the Kingdom that they did not hear Him. Then, when He died, they were dumbfounded. The crucifixion left them confused because of their own preconceived ideas. Now they did not know what to believe. Doubt dominated the disciples. Consequently, they were not shouting the gospel from the housetops; they were sitting silently in their room. When believers doubt, they are dumb. John R. Stott has said that the greatest single reason for the church's evangelistic disobedience is centered in the church's doubts.

Verse 20 says that Christ showed them His hands and His side. Luke informs us that He told them to handle Him (Luke 24:39). The point is, they doubted the resurrection. So before sending them out, He convinced them with a personal appearance and a personal display of His wounds.

THE AUTHORITY FOR THE COMMISSION

After calming and convincing them, Christ commissioned them. He began by stating that the Father had sent Him. Verse 21 says, "As my Father has sent Me, I also send you." *apostellō*, the Greek word for "sent" in the phrase "As the Father has sent Me," refers to official, or authoritative, sending. It is in the perfect tense, indicating that the mission of Christ is not being regarded in its historical fulfillment, but in its permanent effect. B. F. Westcott says, "The form of the fulfillment of Christ's mission was now to be changed, but the mission itself was still to be continued."[1]

pempō, the Greek word translated "send" in the phrase "I also send you," is a general word for sending. It is put in the present tense. The disciples were not to start a new work but were to carry on Christ's work.

The picture painted by this statement is that of a relay runner passing on a baton to another runner. He has received it, has run with it, and now places it in the hand of another, who is to continue the race.

THE POWER FOR THE COMMISSION — THE HOLY SPIRIT

The disciples had been given peace and proof. They had been calmed, convinced, and commissioned, but they were still paralyzed. They were still sitting in the locked room.

So Christ gave them the Holy Spirit. Verse 22 says He breathed on them and said, "Receive the Holy Spirit." Breathing on them was to show that He was imparting to them His very own Spirit.

Whatever occurred here, it was not the baptism of the Holy Spirit, as some have said. By the time of Acts 1:5, forty days after John 20:22, the baptism of the Holy Spirit was still future. In Acts 11:15-16 Peter explains that the Gentiles in Acts 10 had received the baptism of the Holy Spirit "as upon us at the beginning." That means that the beginning of the baptism of the Holy Spirit was on the day of Pentecost as recorded in Acts 2. Therefore, John 20:22 is not referring to the baptism of the Holy Spirit.

Rather, what Jesus bestowed on the disciples at this time was a temporary filling of the Holy Spirit. A. T. Robertson calls this "a foretaste of the great pentecost."[2] John F. Walvoord says, "In John 20:22, apparently a temporary filling of the Spirit was given to provide for their spiritual needs prior to Pentecost. These Gospel passages were not intended to be a norm for the present age, but in general continue the ministry of the Spirit as it had been in the Old Testament."[3]

Though this passage does not say that the Holy Spirit provides the power for evangelism, Luke 24:49 and Acts 1:8 make that abundantly clear. The power is not in the believer's personal peace.

1. 1. B. F. Westcott, *The Gospel According to John*, p. 294.
2. A. T. Robertson, *Word Pictures in the New Testament*, p. 314.
3. John F. Walvoord, *The Holy Spirit*, p. 83.

It is not in his being personally persuaded. It is certainly not in his personality or in his effective presentation. The power is in the person of the Holy Spirit.

THE TASK OF THE COMMISSION — TO FORGIVE AND RETAIN SINS

After breathing on them, Christ said, "If you forgive the sins of any, they are forgiven them; if you retain the sins of any, they are retained." Does that mean Christ gave the apostles the power to forgive and retain sins? No. As Mark 2:7 points out, only God can forgive sins. And Peter did not think this gave him the power to forgive sins, as Acts 8:19–24 clearly demonstrates.

What then does this passage mean? *The Expositor's Greek New Testament* says that it is talking about the ability to "pronounce forgiveness, and to threaten doom."[4] A. T. Robertson expressed it like this: "What he commits to the disciples and to us is the power and privilege of giving assurance of the forgiveness of sins by God by correctly announcing the terms of forgiveness."[5]

There are times when people need to hear a human being tell them, "You are forgiven," or "You are still in your sin." Care must be taken to make sure they understand that only *God* forgives. But the messenger does state it. When I have done this kind of thing, I have guarded myself by saying, "If you have trusted Christ, I can say on the authority of the New Testament you are forgiven," or, "You are entitled to your opinion, but I must warn you that according to the New Testament unless you trust in Christ, you are still in your sin."

By the way, notice that they received the Holy Spirit, which means they had power; and yet verse 23 indicates that they would not always be successful in winning their audience to Christ. Possessing power, even the power of the Holy Spirit, does not guarantee success. Peter was filled with the Holy Spirit and received 3,000 souls. Stephen was filled with the Holy Spirit and received 3,000 stones.

In this context, Christ is in effect saying to the disciples, "With the peace of Christ and the power of the Holy Spirit, you are sent to proclaim forgiveness of sins." As Luke emphasizes the message that we know from the Scriptures, so John's account stresses the power that we obtain from the Holy Spirit.

4. Marcus Dodds, "The Gospel of John," p. 865.
5. A. T. Robertson, *Word Pictures in the New Testament,* p. 315.

6

The Plan

Therefore, when they had come together, they asked Him, saying, "Lord, will You at this time restore the kingdom to Israel?" And He said to them, "It is not for you to know times or seasons which the Father has put in His own authority. But you shall receive power when the Holy Spirit has come upon you; and you shall be witnesses to Me in Jerusalem, and in all Judea and Samaria, and to the end of the earth." Now when He had spoken these things, while they watched, He was taken up, and a cloud received Him out of their sight. And while they looked steadfastly toward heaven as He went up, behold, two men stood by them in white apparel, who also said, "Men of Galilee, why do you stand gazing up into heaven? This same Jesus, who was taken up from you into heaven, will so come in like manner as you saw Him go into heaven." [Acts 1:6–11]

Jesus had been crucified, had risen from the dead, and had appeared to the disciples on several occasions. They were over the shock of His death and the surprise of His resurrection. The fear, the doubt, the unbelief had evaporated. They had been instructed and enlightened. Time had passed, emotions were settled down, and their minds were back on track. Now they had questions.

Of all the questions they could have asked, the one uppermost on their minds was, "Will You at this time restore the kingdom to Israel?" (v. 6). What they had in mind was an earthly, national kingdom. That was the prediction in the Old Testament (Isa. 1:26;

9:7; Jer. 23:5-6; 33:15-17; Dan. 7:13-14; Hos. 3:4-5; Amos 9:11; Zech. 9:9). That was the expectation of the nation. Richard B. Rackham says, "They retain the old Jewish idea of the Messianic 'kingdom of God' as a glorious empire of Israel."[1] Richard C. H. Lenski states, "They thought of a glorious earthly rule for Israel."[2] F.F. Bruce calls this their "hope of an earthly and national kingdom."[3]

Jesus answered their question and corrected their thinking. In verse 7 He told them, "It is not for you to know"—literally, "It is not given you to know." Bruce paraphrases this, "It is not your concern."[4] We would say, "It is none of your business." In essence, Jesus said, "That's later. It's not your concern now."

Evidently, they did not have the wrong concept of the kingdom. It was just that the kingdom was not to be their concern now. The kingdom was future. Other matters must concern them at this time. Believers today still have a tendency to get sidetracked. They get stuck on side issues and minor matters. Two of the most popular are the extreme past and the extreme future: the creation story of Genesis 1 and the Millennium of Revelation 20. The point is not that those things are not true, or not important. They are. But they are not the major concern now.

THE TASK OF THE COMMISSION – TO SPEAK

Their main concern was not to be prophecy but preaching the gospel. Verse 8 says, "You shall be witnesses to Me."

Is witnessing something one is or something one does? Years ago I heard a preacher suggest that witnessing was something a person *was.* He used Acts 1:8 and the words "You shall *be*" to prove it. His point was that what we are is more important that what we say. But although what we are is important in evangelism, technically, evangelism is something one does. The Greek word for witnessing, *martureō,* is a forensic term from the courtroom that implies—yea, demands—speaking. Imagine a witness in the courtroom who says nothing. The judge would hold him in contempt of the court.

If the redeemed of the Lord do not say so, the world will credit them with having commendable moral behavior instead of glorifying

---

1. Richard B. Rackham, *The Acts of the Apostles,* p.7.
2. Richard C.H. Lenski, *The Interpretation of the Acts of the Apostles,* p. 29.
3. F.F. Bruce, *The Acts of the Apostles,* p. 70.
4. Ibid.

God. Silent believers are like beautiful road signs with no words printed on them. Your lips, as well as your life, must speak of Christ; verse 8 says they were to be witnesses *"to Me,"* that is, Christ.

What is included in witnessing about Christ? Is it telling sinners about His life, His lectures, His miracles, His marvels? Or, does it mean primarily His death and resurrection? Luke 24:48 says, "And you are witnesses of these things." The context clearly indicates that "these things" were Christ's death and resurrection. So when Christ told the disciples (v. 8) that they were to be "witnesses to Me," He meant that they were to tell people about His death and resurrection. The task is not to tell people about your church, or your conversion, or your creed, but Christ. Further, in talking about Him, the primary focus must be His death for sin and His resurrection from the dead.

THE POWER OF THE COMMISSION – IT MUST BE USED

Christ wanted the disciples to witness, but not without the Holy Spirit. The reason is obvious: the Holy Spirit provides the power for evangelism. Verse 8 says, "You shall receive power when the Holy Spirit has come upon you." The reception of power is simultaneous with the coming of the Holy Spirit, not subsequent to it. This is a reference to the baptism of the Holy Spirit mentioned earlier (v. 5), which all Christians after Pentecost receive at conversion (1 Cor. 12:13). Thus, if you have trusted Christ, you have the Holy Spirit and you have the power of the Holy Spirit.

A believer may not feel that power, but he has it. The word "power" *(dunamis)* simply means the ability to perform. When a Christian witnesses concerning the cross of Christ, the Holy Spirit has the ability to effect conviction and conversion. With gas in the tank a driver has power, that is, the ability to perform. If he waits until he feels the power, he will never move. But if he starts the engine and pushes the pedal, he will experience the power. Likewise, a believer should not wait until he feels power. He should start to witness, and then he will experience the power at work.

THE PLAN OF THE COMMISSION

The Lord also told the disciples where to witness. They were to begin at Jerusalem, that is, where they were, and go beyond, extending to the ends of the earth. Jerusalem was the capital city of Judea. Judea was the province. Samaria was the next neighboring province. "The end of the earth" signifies that they were to go as far as the most remote country.

The order is important since it assures that there will be evangelism at home and evangelism abroad, commonly called missions. If the order is reversed, a church will have strong mission support but weak home evangelism.

His discourse was finished; it was not interrupted by His departure. But upon the completion of His charge, He was "taken up"— literally, lifted or raised up. The latter part of verse 9 informs us that a cloud received Him out of their sight. Many commentaries take the cloud to be a symbol of the Shekinah glory, that is, the very presence of God. The one thing that is for sure is that the body of Christ was removed from the eyes of the apostles. They were to cease looking up.

The commission given in verse 8 is the last utterance of Jesus Christ before His ascension. Thus He is telling us that evangelism, not prophecy, is to be our major concern. The last thing a coach tells his players before they run out on the field; the last instruction of the general before the battle; the last lesson of the teacher before graduation; surely these are significant. The alert leader makes sure that his last words underscore what is to be the major concern.

As they were staring intently, even straining their eyes, they were startled by the appearance of two men. The fact that they were dressed in white apparel has led many to conclude that these were angels in human form. In Luke 24:4, Luke does call angels "men," and white apparel does appear to be the color of angels' garb (Matt. 18:3; John 20:12).

The creatures, whether heavenly or earthly, were messengers. Their communication was short, like a telegram: "This same Jesus, who was taken up from you into heaven, will so come in like manner as you saw Him go into heaven." He went away visibly, ascending into clouds. He shall return in clouds. He was received into heaven; He shall return from heaven.

This reminder must have reinforced the importance of the task. They were told to witness to the whole world, and then Christ immediately disappeared. That underscored in their minds that witnessing was to be of major importance. Then they were reminded that he is coming back. Surely one of the first things to occur to them was the thought *And when He gets back, He is going to want to know if we did what He told us to do*. Dramatically, the Lord impressed upon them the significance of this demand.

7

Again, Why Evangelize?

If a study were done of Christians who are evangelistic, the result would probably reveal that most are involved for one of three reasons.

(1) New converts are usually evangelistic because of their conversion experience. Out of the excitement and emotion of their new-found faith, they tell others about Christ. Andrew is a biblical illustration. John 1:41 tells us that after his experience with Christ he first found his own brother and said to him, "We have found the Messiah." That is good; but the excitement soon wears off.

(2) Older Christians are sometimes involved in evangelism because of a training program. They are enlisted and enrolled in a short-term evangelistic seminar. In conjunction with the classes they are assigned to communicate the gospel, and they do. That is good; but the program or class ends and, in the majority of cases, so does the soul-winning.

(3) Some saints are forced into evangelistic activity by guilt. A preacher tells them that the lost are hell-bound. Christians, he says, must warn the lost. If they don't, the blood of non-Christians will be on their heads. Thus, driven by guilt, the believer tells others about heaven. That is not so good. It is true that the lost are headed for hell. Granted, Christians are responsible to give them the good news about Christ. But if the motivation is guilt or fear, that is less than what God wants.

Those are a few of the reasons that some are evangelistic. But why should Christians evangelize? What is the biblical basis for evangelism? A summary of all five passages on the Great Commission will give us the biblical answer to that question.

No one passage of the five gives all the elements of the Great Commission. Matthew and John record the authority for the Commission. Matthew, Mark, and Luke include the extent of the Commission. Matthew, Luke, and John inform us that the Holy Spirit is the power for the Commission. Mark mentions the message, and Luke adds details. Only Mark and Luke discuss the message. Mark alone relates the confirmation of the Commission.

Of course, all five passages mention the task. Yet, there is not uniformity even here. Matthew says the task is to make disciples. Mark's passage demands that we preach the gospel to every creature. Luke's version is that repentance and remission of sins is to be preached in all the world. According to John, the task is to forgive and retain sins. And Acts says the disciples are to be witnesses concerning Christ.

George W. Peters says, "No one of them gives it [the Great Commission] in all of its completeness. But they beautifully supplement each other. While each of the evangelists presents it from his own point of view, and with his own unique emphasis, together they make a complete whole. . . . Only as we see the whole outline, as presented in the four gospels, do we see the total Great Commission."[1]

THE TOTAL TASK

Only Matthew gives us the all-inclusive Great Commission. According to the Lord's words as recorded by Matthew, the Great Commission is by the authority of Christ, and the disciples were to go into all the world and make disciples in the power of the Holy Spirit. The all-inclusive, total task of the Great Commission is to make disciples. As a study of that passage reveals, discipling includes evangelizing, baptizing, and teaching.

THE EVANGELISTIC EMPHASIS

Although the total program includes baptizing and teaching, a

1. G. W. Peters, *A Biblical Theology of Missions*, p. 174.

study of all five passages reveals that the emphasis of the Great Commission is on evangelism. The command in Mark is to preach the gospel. The commission in Luke is to preach repentance and remission of sins. The charge in John is to forgive and retain sins. And, as Luke reminds us in Acts 1, just before He left, the Lord communicated again to them that they were to witness concerning Him to the very ends of the earth. The ultimate goal may be spiritual maturity and the total task may include teaching, but clearly the emphasis of the Great Commission is on evangelism.

THE BIBLICAL BASIS OF EVANGELISM

Believers evangelize because they are commanded to as part of the all-inclusive task of the total Great Commission. Evangelism is not optional, it is imperative. There is no way to fulfill the Great Commission without evangelizing. Believers evangelize because God commanded them to do so.

Some would say that we are to evangelize because of the need of men. They are lost and going to hell. We have the message that will save them, so we must give the message to them. Granted, the Bible teaches that men are without light and headed for outer darkness, but the New Testament does not use that as the reason for evangelism.[2]

The reason for evangelism is the command of God, not the condition of men. No doubt, contemplating the miserable mess men are in could move us to minister to them. That is emotional motivation. But when our stirred emotions settle down, wear off, or grow old, the emotional motivation dies.

God commands—make disciples. That involves evangelism. But the issue is not emotional. God demands our rational, volitional action. We are to evangelize not because we want to or because we like to, nor because we choose to, but because we are told to.

I could get my son to mow the lawn by pointing out the need.

---

2. The question could be raised, "But what if Christians do not evangelize? Will people go to hell because they were not given the gospel?" This is a serious question, but it is not the most important matter confronting us. The point of this chapter is that we evangelize not because of the condition of men, but because of the commandment of God. Frankly, whether people are going to hell or not isn't the issue. God has commanded us to evangelize. That is the issue.

I can just see it now. I could plead, "Oh, son, see the grass? It's in terrible shape. It needs cutting." I could then wait for him to see the need and cut the grass. Frankly, that has worked. But it has also not worked, depending on the mood of my son. Now, my son does mow the lawn, but the reason is because his father says, "Go mow the lawn." That is not to deny that the need is there. It is just to say that the reason is the command of his father.

God's children need to be reminded that the Father has given them a command!

Part 3

The Message in Evangelism

8

The Bad News That Is Good News

The subject of this chapter is sin. For many, that is bad news.
But this is a case of the bad news being good news.

Sin is part and parcel of the message in evangelism. After the
Lord arose and before He ascended, He gave the disciples the
Great Commission. A careful consideration of the passages that
record the Great Commission will reveal that sin is to be preached.
Note:

> If you forgive the sins of any, they are forgiven them; if you retain
> the sins of any, they are retained. (John 20:23)

> And that repentance and remission of sins should be preached in
> His name to all nations, beginning at Jerusalem. (Luke 24:47)

Think of it! The Lord wants us to talk to others about sin. That
is the bad news. Sin is bad news; and talking to others about their
sin is worse. The subject sounds bad, but this is a case in which
the bad news is really good news. A thorough understanding of
the subject of sin will demonstrate that such is the case.

THEOLOGICAL DEFINITION OF SIN

Theologians define sin as anything contrary to the nature of God.
Crime is that which is against government; sin is that which is

against God. There are several different aspects of sin.

Imputed sin. Scholars point out that Adam's sin was imputed to the whole human race. Paul says, "Therefore, just as through one man sin entered the world, and death through sin, and thus death spread to all men, because all sinned" (Rom. 5:12). In Adam's fall, all fell. As our representatives in Congress pass laws that are imputed to us, so Adam, as our representative, did something thousands of years ago in another place that is imputed to us today.

Inherent sin. Theologians talk about inherent sin as well. When Adam sinned, his very nature became corrupt; and thus, every descendant of Adam inherited the Adamic, corrupt, depraved, sinful nature. Ephesians 2:3 states that we are all sinners by nature. Man is totally depraved. He has a darkened mind, depraved emotions, and a disobedient will.

Individual sins. Theology professors also talk about individual sins. Individual sins are simply those personal sins all people commit, either intentionally or unintentionally. All individuals commit such sins. See Romans 3:12–18 for Paul's description of personal sins. This category includes murder, adultery, stealing, and lying.

The point is that sin is anything contrary to the nature of God. Does that mean that the message in evangelism must include a discussion of imputed and inherent sin? Not necessarily. Paul did not use the theological concept of sin to prove to a lost man that he was a sinner. He used the theological idea as an introduction to the doctrine of sanctification.

Consider the outline of Romans:

Romans 1:1–17	Introduction
Romans 1:18–3:20	Condemnation
Romans 3:21–5:11	Justification
Romans 5:12–21	Transition
Romans 6–8	Sanctification

Where does Paul talk about imputed sin? In Romans 5:12–21, *after* he has discussed justification. Thus Paul did not use the *theological* concept of sin to get a sinner saved, but in preparation for getting a saint sanctified.

Well then, how did Paul communicate the message of sin to men without Christ.

PRACTICAL COMMUNICATION OF SIN

The way to communicate the concept of sin to an unsaved person is by the use of the law. Paul said of himself (Rom. 7:7) that except for the law he would not have known sin. When he wrote his great theological treatise on salvation, he said that the knowledge of sin is by the law (Rom. 3:20). He even declared that those without the law—that is, the Gentiles—had the law written on their hearts (Rom. 2:15). Paul shows us that in order to communicate the concept of sin to a sinner, we should use the law. After all, the law is not for a righteous man, but for sinners (1 Tim. 1:9).

Christ followed the same practice. He used the law to prove to a lost man that he was a sinner. The rich young ruler came to Christ and asked how he might inherit eternal life (Mark 10:17–23). Christ began by talking about Himself. He asked, "Why do you call Me good? No one is good but One, that is, God" (v. 18). In other words, He was asking, "Are you calling me God?" The young fellow did not respond, so Christ brought up the law. He said, "You know the commandments" (v. 19). Christ did not get theological. He simply used the law to prove to the rich young ruler that he had broken the law and thus was a sinner.

Does that mean that in evangelism one must start with the law or always use the Ten Commandments? Again, not necessarily.

EVANGELISM AND SIN

There are times when a witness for Christ may start somewhere else to show a sinner his need. The gospel of John was written to get people saved. Yet it does not talk a great deal about the Ten Commandments; it centers on Christ. In his book *How to Give Away Your Faith,* Paul Little suggests that the "I am" designations in the gospel of John are designed to reveal to modern man his need.[1]

Emptiness. In John 6:35 Jesus says, "I am the bread of life." Man is empty and hungry. Jesus satisfies. Most people know they are empty, or at least that they are not satisfied, so they try to fill their lives with possessions, pleasure, and power. Or they shovel in self-made or man-made righteousness. But it does not work. It doesn't satisfy. It is like eating junk food instead of steak. Jesus satisfies

---

1. Paul Little, *How to Give Away Your Faith,* p. 57.

the emptiness inside like a salad, a baked potato, and a filet mignon satisfies a hungry man.

Purposelessness. In John 8:12 Jesus says, "I am the light of the world." Man is in darkness and does not know where he is going. He is aimless and purposeless. It is like being caught in a dark room. Without light, a person gropes around trying to find the light switch. He bumps into things. He brushes against something. He breaks something. If something were to bump against him, his heart would sink to his toes. Finally, he finds the switch; the light comes on; he can see. He knows where he is and can see where he is going. Likewise, Jesus is the Light of the world. Once in the light, a person understands life. He has purpose and direction.

Loneliness. In John 10:11 Jesus says, "I am the good shepherd." Man is separated from God and is thus alone, alienated from others. But when Jesus is the shepherd, a person is never alone. For Jesus said, "I will never leave you nor forsake you." Furthermore, a shepherd has a flock. When one is a member of a flock, he is not only related to the shepherd, but to the rest of the flock, and thus he is not alone.

To sum up: theologically, sin is anything contrary to the law of God. Practically, sin is breaking the Ten Commandments. Psychologically, man has a need, or a lack. The message of sin is indispensable to evangelism, but be practical and evangelistic— in short, don't get theological. Use God's law, *or* man's lack to show sinners their need.

Sin is bad news. Yet, this bad news is good news. Sin is good news because sin is solvable. Modern man has been brainwashed into thinking his problem is not in himself: his problem is his parents, or his peers, his boss, neighbors, or the government. It is not inside him, but outside. If that were the case, man would be without hope, for there would be no solution. But when he sees that his problem is sin, then there is hope, for that problem can be solved, and that is the good news.

Sin is also good news because it is the truth, and people appreciate being told the truth. If a person is told that he is a sinner in a self-righteous, condemning manner, he will not like it. But if someone identifies with him by saying "I too am a sinner," then graciously instructs him, "You are a sinner," and finally informs him that Christ is the solution, he will not be offended. If he gets the message and trusts Christ, he will be eternally grateful. People want to know the truth. They want a doctor who tells them the truth, a lawyer who levels with them, a mechanic who is honest; and in spiritual matters, they want the truth.

I once counseled with a heavy-set housewife who was having some difficulties with her husband. I listened to her tale of woe, and I listened, and I listened, and I listened. After several hours she asked, "Well, what do you think?" I calmly looked at her and said, "Well, for starters, you're fat. You need to lose weight." Her immediate response was, "Thank you. You're the first person who has ever been honest with me. When I buy a new dress my friends say, 'Oh, it looks great.' And I know they're lying. I'm fat. I can't look great in anything. Thanks for your honesty."

We need to tell people the truth about sin. They will appreciate it, and God will be pleased, since that is what He told us to do.

9

What Is the Gospel?

Jesus Christ issued a jumbo-sized job for believers: to go into all the world and preach the gospel to every creature. Obviously, if this job is to be done, the job must be understood. It is not difficult to understand going into all the world or preaching to every creature. But what about the gospel? What is the gospel?

That may sound like asking the obvious. Everyone understands the gospel—right? No. Wrong. Many have misunderstood the gospel of the grace of God. D.L. Moody, the nineteenth-century Billy Graham, is reported to have said, "I think I had been a partaker of the gospel ten years before I knew what the word meant."

Diverse opinions exist on what the gospel is. A gospel singer being interviewed on radio is asked to give his testimony. He says, "I was unloved, rejected, alone, and lonely. I suffered from an inferiority complex. I struggled with insecurity. Then I heard the gospel. I heard God loves me. God's love changed my life." Is that the gospel? The proclamation at the fifth assembly of the World Council of Churches in Nairobi said, "The Gospel always includes the responsibility to participate in the struggle for justice and human dignity, the obligation to denounce all that hinders human wholeness."[1] Is that the gospel?

Just what *is* the gospel?

1. Harold Lindsell, "Nairobi: Crisis and Credibility," pp. 11–12.

THE GOSPEL IN THE NEW TESTAMENT

The Greek word translated "gospel" *(euangelion)* means good news." In secular Greek, it was a general term for any good news. In Scripture, it is more specific—it is a technical term for the good news of Christ. Yet even in the New Testament, *euangelion* is used in different senses.

For example, John the Baptist announces the gospel of the coming kingdom. The "gospel of the kingdom" (Mark 1:14–15) is the good news that the Messiah will come to set up His kingdom as prophesied in the Old Testament. The four gospels primarily, and the book of Acts to some degree, deal with this gospel.

The "gospel of the grace of God" (Acts 20:24) is described in more detail in the epistles. There is only one passage in the New Testament that defines that gospel, 1 Corinthians 15:1–8. The subject of 1 Corinthians 15 is the resurrection. There were people in the church at Corinth who were denying the resurrection of the dead (v. 12). Evidently they did not reject the resurrection of Christ, just the resurrection of the dead. So Paul begins with the resurrection of Christ and argues from that to the resurrection of believers.

Even though the subject of 1 Corinthians 15 is really the resurrection of believers, Paul begins with the gospel. The first eight verses can be divided into two parts: first, Paul tells them that he is going to declare unto them the gospel he preached and they received. This is the gospel by which they were saved (vv. 1–2). Then he defines that gospel (vv. 3–8). Since the ultimate purpose of the chapter is to deal with the resurrection, Paul spends the bulk of this part of the passage on proving the resurrection. But his definition of the gospel is clear: Christ died for our sins, and Christ arose from the dead.

What then is the relationship between the gospel of the kingdom and the gospel of the grace of God? There are three possibilities. (1) The gospel of the kingdom and the gospel of the grace of God are two different things. In the original Scofield Bible one note says, "Four forms of the gospel are to be distinguished . . ."[2] (2) The gospel of the kingdom and the gospel of the grace of God are identical. F. F. Bruce, in his commentary on Acts, says, "It [the gospel of the kingdom of God] is identical with the 'gospel of the grace of

2. *Scofield Reference Bible,* p. 1343.

God.' "³ (3) The gospel of the kingdom and the gospel of the grace of God are not two different things (that is, separate and unrelated), nor one thing (that is, identical), but are two parts of the same thing.

My understanding is that the two can be distinguished, but not divorced. The gospel of the kingdom is the good news that Christ, the King, has come to set up His kingdom. The gospel of the grace of God is that God saves sinners by His grace. Thus, the gospel of the kingdom includes the gospel of the grace of God.

THE GOSPEL IN EVANGELISM

Now the question is, Which of these "gospels" is to be preached in evangelism? Mark 16:15 says, "Preach the gospel." But what exactly did Jesus have in mind? Mark 1:14–15 says that John preached the gospel of the kingdom. Mark 13:10 teaches that the gospel of the kingdom must be preached in all the world before Christ returns. Is the gospel of the kingdom the message in evangelism today?

No. The gospel of the kingdom is to be taught today, and it will be preached during the Tribulation period, which precedes the second coming of Christ; but the message in evangelism today is the gospel of the grace of God. Granted, John the Baptist and Jesus began preaching the gospel of the kingdom. But later, Jesus prepared the disciples for the message of the gospel of the grace of God (see Mark 8:27–31). Furthermore, when Jesus said, "Preach the gospel to every creature" (Mark 16:15), He meant the good news of His death and resurrection, that is, the gospel of the grace of God. It is obvious that He had that in mind. For one thing, the word *gospel* was used in Mark of the death of Christ (Mark 14:9). But more important, in the context of the several utterances of the Great Commission, Jesus made it clear that they were to preach His death and resurrection.

Peter preached the death and resurrection of Christ on the day of Pentecost (Acts 2:24, 32) and again when the lame man was healed (3:12–15). He proclaimed that same message to the Gentiles (10:37–41). Paul also habitually preached that identical message (17:2–3). Paul's habitual practice was to preach the gospel of the grace of God.

After a Bible study, a lawyer once said to me, "Isn't all the Bible

3. F.F. Bruce, *The Acts of the Apostles,* pp. 185–6.

good news? Therefore, all the Bible is the gospel." Obviously, there
is some truth to that, but the good news *in evangelism* is that Christ
died for our sins and arose from the dead. That God created the
world and man may be good news, but that good news will not get
anyone saved.

THE GOSPEL TO BE PREACHED TODAY

The conclusion is obvious. The "gospel of the grace of God" was
the message in evangelism in the first century and should be our
message today. But in many circles that is not the case. Some mix the
gospel of the grace of God with social activism and call it all
"gospel." For example, the World Council of Churches' declaration
that "the gospel always includes the responsibility to participate in
the struggle for justice and human dignity, the obligation to
denounce all that hinders human wholeness"[4] is simply not true. In
the practice of the apostles in Acts, and the precepts of the apostles
in the epistles, the gospel *never* included social activism. That is not
to say that Christians should not help the poor, nor be involved in
social concern; it is to insist that such activity is not part of the gospel
or the Great Commission.

Harold Lindsell's reaction to the Nairobi conference expresses it
well:

> Section I devoted itself to this matter and brought back a report that
> was considerably better than anything coming out of Mexico City,
> Uppsala or Bangkok. It called for the proclamation of the whole Gospel
> to the whole world by the whole church. "We are called to preach
> Christ crucified, and risen again," it said. The proclamation includes
> "the announcement of God's Kingdom and the love through Jesus
> Christ, the offer of grace and forgiveness of sins, the invitation to
> repentance and faith in Him, the summons to fellowship in God's
> church."
>
> Regrettably, the thrust of this statement was blunted somewhat by
> the inclusion of the insertion that the Gospel "always includes the
> responsibility to participate in the struggle for human dignity, the
> obligation to denounce all that hinders human wholeness." These
> things are not an intrinsic part of the Gospel; they are a part of the total
> mission of the Christian witness and should neither be obscured nor
> overlooked. The essence of the Gospel lies in its vertical dimension, in

4. Lindsell, "Nairobi," pp. 11–12.

which man is made righteous in the eyes of God, which is followed by a new horizontal perspective, in which man is made right with his fellow man. The struggle for justice and human wholeness is a logical and irresistible outgrowth of the new birth.[5]

The gospel we must preach today is not the social gospel to reform society, but the gospel of God to redeem sinners.

Others miss it altogether. They preach around the gospel. They believe the gospel, but they do not proclaim it clearly. Many evangelicals today are not preaching the gospel of the grace of God—they are preaching the gospel of God's love. The whole "pitch" of their message is: "God loves you and you need to accept God's love." There is no mention of sin, the cross, or the resurrection of Christ.

In a day when parents are too busy to spend time with their children, the children feel unloved and respond to the emotional presentation of love. Obviously it is true that God loves us and, for that matter, the whole world. But preaching God's love minus God's grace is not gospel preaching.

The Great Commission demanded and the apostles practiced preaching the gospel of the grace of God, that is, that Christ died for sins and arose from the dead. When we evangelize we must tell people exactly that. Like the two wings of a bird or the two rails of a track, both the death and resurrection of Christ are necessary and important.

Let me illustrate how the gospel should be preached. Charles Haddon Spurgeon gave his own testimory of conversion as follows.

> While under the concern of soul, I resolved that I would attend all the places of worship in the town where I lived, in order that I might find out the way of salvation. I was willing to do anything, and be anything, if God would only forgive my sin. I set off, determined to go round to all the chapels, and I did go to every place of worship; but for a long time I went in vain. I do not, however, blame the ministers. One man preached Divine Sovereignty; I could hear him with pleasure, but what was that sublime truth to a poor sinner who wished to know what he must do to be saved? There was another admirable man who always preached about the law, but what was the use of ploughing up ground that needed to be sown? Another was a practical preacher. I heard him,

5. Ibid., pp. 11–12.

but it was very much like a commanding officer teaching the manoeuvres of war to a set of men without feet. What could I do? All his exhortations were lost on me. I knew it was said "Believe on the Lord Jesus Christ, and thou shalt be saved," but I did not know what it was to believe on Christ.

I sometimes think I might have been in darkness and despair until now had it not been for the goodness of God in sending a snowstorm, one Sunday morning, while I was going to a certain place of worship. When I could go no further, I turned down a side street, and came to a little Primitive Methodist Chapel. In that chapel there may have been a dozen or fifteen people. . . . The minister did not come that morning; he was snowed up, I suppose. At last, a very thin-looking man, a shoemaker, or tailor, or something of that sort, went up into the pulpit to preach. Now, it is well that preachers should be instructed, but this man was really stupid. He was obliged to stick to his text, for the simple reason that he had little else to say. The text was—

"LOOK UNTO ME, AND BE YE SAVED, ALL THE ENDS OF THE EARTH." He did not even pronounce the words rightly, but that did not matter. There was, I thought, a glimpse of hope for me in that text. The preacher began thus: "My dear friends, this is a very simple text indeed. It says, 'Look.' Now lookin' don't take a deal of pain. It ain't liftin' your foot or your finger; it is just, 'Look.' Well, a man needn't go to College to learn to look. You may be the biggest fool, and yet you can look. A man needn't be worth a thousand a year to be able to look. Anyone can look; even a child can look. But then the text says, 'Look unto *Me.*' Ay!" said he, in broad Essex, "many on ye are lookin' to yourselves, but it's no use lookin' there. You'll never find any comfort in yourselves. Some look to God the Father. No, look to Him by-and-by. Jesus Christ says, 'Look unto *Me.*' Some on ye say, 'We must wait for the Spirit's workin'.' You have no business with that just now. Look to *Christ.* The text says, 'Look unto *Me.*' "

Then the good man followed up his text in this way; "Look unto Me; I am sweatin' great drops of blood. Look unto Me; I am hangin' on the cross. Look unto Me; I am dead and buried. Look unto Me; I rise again. Look unto Me; I ascend to Heaven. Look unto Me; I am sittin' at the Father's right hand. O poor sinner, look unto Me! Look unto Me!"

When he had gone to about that length, and managed to spin out ten minutes or so, he was at the end of his tether. Then he looked at me under the gallery, and I daresay, with so few present, he knew me to be a stranger. Just fixing his eyes on me, as if he knew all my heart, he said, "Young man, you look very miserable." Well, I did, but I had not been accustomed to have remarks made from the pulpit on my personal appearance before. However, it was a good blow, struck right home. He continued, "and you always will be miserable—miserable in life, and miserable in death—if you don't obey my text; but if you obey now, this moment, you will be saved." Then, lifting up his hands, he shouted, as only a Primitive Methodist could do, "Young man, look to Jesus Christ. Look! Look! Look!" . . .Oh! I looked until I could almost have looked my eyes away. There and then the cloud was gone, the darkness had rolled away, and that moment I saw the sun; and I could have risen that instant, and sung with the most enthusiastic of them, of the precious blood of Christ, and the simple faith which looks alone to Him. Oh, that somebody had told me this before, "Trust Christ, and you shall be saved."[6]

That, my friend, is *gospel* preaching!

6. Charles H. Spurgeon, *The Early Years*, pp. 86–88.

10
What Is Repentance?

Ask three Christian leaders to define repentance and you will probably get three different answers. Dr. Lewis Sperry Chafer says, "The word means a *change of mind*," and again, "The true meaning of the word shows that it is a change of mind."[1] Dr. R.P. Shuller insists that it contains tears: "I believe in a repentance baptized by weeping. For myself, I pray that I may see the day again when men and women will fall, as of yore at the altars of prayer, crying to God for mercy and interpreting their grief in penitential tears."[2] Many evangelists preaching on repentance define it as a change of life. They say something like, "Unless you have turned from your evil ways, unless there has been a marked change in your manner of living, you have never truly repented, for to repent means to change." Now, which leader is correct? What is repentance?

This is an important question. The Lord Himself commanded that repentance be preached in all the world (Luke 24:47). God commands all men, Jews and Gentiles, everywhere to repent (Acts 17:30). Obviously, then, repentance is necessary for salvation. As Chafer has stated, "Therefore, it is as dogmatically stated as language can declare, that repentance is essential to salvation and that none

1. Lewis Sperry Chafer, *Systematic Theology*, 3:372; 7:265.
2. R.P. Shuller, "The Way," p. 1.

could be saved, apart from repentance."[3] If we must repent to be saved, then we must preach repentance. But first we must know what repentance is.

THE MEANING OF REPENTANCE

Repentance is basically a change of mind. *Metanoia*, the Greek word translated "repent," is a compound made up of two definite Greek words. The first is *meta*, "after," and the second is *noēma*, "mind." Thus, the two together mean "afterthought," or "change of mind." The word describes an inward change of thinking or attitude. Julius R. Mantey says, "It means to think differently or have a different attitude toward sin and God, etc."[4] Bishop Westcott in his commentary on Hebrews 6:1 says, "It follows, therefore, that 'Repentance *from* dead works' expresses that complete change of mind—of spiritual attitude—which leads the believer to abandon these works and seek some other support for life."[5] Alfred Plummer in his comment on Luke 3:3 calls repentance "an inward change of mind."[6]

When someone changes his mind, there may be emotions—and there may not be. And when someone changes his mind, a change in his course of action is expected. But both of these things are *results* of repentance, and not the nature of repentance.

Repentance is *not* being sorry for sin. This is the popular idea of repentance. Some even insist on tears. Robert Smith said, "True repentance has a double aspect. It looks upon things past with a weeping eye, and upon the future with a watchful eye."[7] There is even a tradition that the lily sprang from the repentant tears of Eve as she went forth from paradise. Most do not carry the idea of remorse that far, but many do feel that repentance is being sorry for sin, and that is simply not the case.

Paul plainly demonstrates that sorrow and repentance are two different things: "your sorrow led to repentance" (2 Cor. 7:9). Sorrow may lead to repentance; sorrow may accompany repentance; but sorrow is not repentance. There is another Greek word,

---

3. Chafer, 3:373.
4. Julius R. Mantey, "Repentance and Conversion," p. 193.
5. B.F. Westcott, *The Epistle to the Hebrews*, p. 144.
6. Alfred Plummer, *A Critical and Exegetical Commentary on the Gospel According to Luke*, p. 86.
7. Paul Lee Tan, *Encyclopedia of 7,700 Illustrations*, p. 1133.

metamelomai, which means "to regret," and that Greek word is never used in a salvation passage. There is an obvious difference between regretting and repenting. In Acts 2 the Jews regretted what they did to Christ and asked, "What shall we do?" (v. 37). It was after their regret that Peter said, "Repent" (v. 38).

There is a sorrow that does not lead to repentance. In 2 Corinthians 7:10 Paul goes on to say, "Godly sorrow produces repentance to salvation, not to be regretted; but the sorrow of the world produces death." One can be sorry and have that sorrow prompt him to change his mind, or one can be sorry and have that sorrow produce a hard heart.

During my college and seminary days I preached in jails and prisons. I met many men who said they were sorry. But as I talked with them I realized that they were not sorry for what they had done. Rather, they were sorry that they had been caught. Sorrow may lead to repentance, and it may not.

One other observation: sorrow does not have to precede repentance. Paul says the goodness of God can also lead to repentance (Rom. 2:4). D. L. Moody used to say that the inquirer is not to seek sorrow, but the Savior.

Repentance is not turning from sin. That is another common misunderstanding. One fiery preacher may thunder, "Repentance, which was the burden of the Baptist's message, involves the sense of sorrow, sorrow for sin, and the severance from sin by the grace and power of God. He who repents realizes that he is a sinner, regrets his sin and resolves to forsake it. Remember: he that lacks time to mourn lacks time to mend." "Turn or burn" is their message. Eloquently, and even poetically, they proclaim:

> 'Tis not enough to say,
> "I'm sorry and repent"
> And then go on from day to day,
> Just as I always went.
>
> Repentance is to leave
> The sins we loved before,
> And show that we in earnest grieve
> By doing them no more.[8]

8. Walter B. Knight, *Master Book of Illustrations*, p. 542.

Publicly, and in personal evangelism, this is the message often preached.

In an evangelism booklet entitled "Step Up to Life," Elmer H. Murdoch says, "Repentance is a deep change of mind and heart which leads you to reject and forsake all known sin and the right to run your life independently of God . . . . Repentance is a spiritual U-turn necessary before you believe."[9]

But Acts 26:20 clearly demonstrates that repenting and turning are two different things. Paul says in that verse that the Gentiles should "repent *and* turn to God" (literal translation). Luke 17:1-4 is an illustration that proves the point. Jesus teaches that if a man repents seven times in one day, he is to be forgiven seven times. There is no question that there is genuine repentance here—the whole point assumes that the repentance is genuine. Yet this genuine repentance did not affect his conduct. Roger Post says of this passage that it "implies that in the word 'repent' itself a change of conduct or an alteration of one's lifestyle is not required."[10]

The fact that repentance is not turning from sin explains why the New Testament repeatedly talks about repenting *and* bringing forth fruit fit for repentance (Luke 3:8, Acts 26:20). Lenski in his commentary on Luke 3:8 points out that "repentance cannot be meant by 'fruits' . . . . 'Fruits' indicate an organic connection between themselves and repentance just as the tree brings the fruit that is particular to its nature . . . . [Repentance] is invisible; hence, we judge its presence by the [fruits], which are invisible."[11]

L. Berkhoff says, "According to Scripture repentance is wholly an inward act, and should not be confounded with the change of life that proceeds from it. Confession of sin and reparation of wrongs are *fruits* of repentance."[12] In other words, the result of repentance *should* be a change in action; but the change in action is the fruit, not the essence, of repentance.

The conclusive evidence that repentance does not mean to be sorry for sin or to turn from sin is this: in the Old Testament, *God* repents. In the King James Version, the word *repent* occurs forty-six times in the Old Testament. Thirty-seven of these times,

9. Elmer H. Murdoch, *Step Up to Life*, pp. 10-11.
10. Roger Post, "The Meanings of the Words Translated 'Repent' and 'Repentance' in the New Testament," pp. 66-67.
11. Richard C.H. Lenski, *The Interpretation of St. Luke's Gospel*, p. 188.
12. L. Berkhoff, *Systematic Theology*, p. 487.

God is the one repenting (or not repenting). If repentance meant sorrow for *sin*, God would be a sinner.

The conclusion is clear. Repentance means a change of mind or attitude. It does not include tears or turning. It doesn't even necessarily deal with sin. (As a matter of fact, "Plutarch tells of two murderers, who having spared a child, afterwards 'repented' and sought to slay it.")[13] If someone changes his mind, a change in behavior should result, but the word *repent* looks at the change of belief, not the change in behavior.

THE OBJECTS OF REPENTANCE

To clarify the meaning even more, the objects, or concerns, of repentance must be understood. It is commonly assumed that repentance always deals with sin. But again, that is not the case. The word means a change of mind or attitude—period. The matter one changes his mind about is not in or implied by the word. The different view held by the repentant person may concern God or man, fishing or eating, sin or sun-bathing.

Let me illustrate. What does "dozen" mean? A farmer would say twelve eggs. A baker would insist that it is twelve donuts. Now, does "dozen" mean twelve *eggs* or twelve *donuts*? The answer is neither. It simply means twelve—period. The context (the farm or the bakery) determines its object.

What is the object of repentance in the New Testament? There are several. God is sometimes the object (Acts 20:21). If a person has a wrong concept of God, he must repent, that is, change his mind about God. If he believes that God is an idol, he must repent and see that the true and living God is the invisible creator of the universe. If he believes that God is a mean, arbitrary judge, he must repent and see that God is just, yet merciful; He is gracious and loving, as well as righteous.

Another object of repentance is Christ. This one is not so much stated as implied. In Acts 2 Peter preached that the Jews had the wrong view of Christ. They thought of Him as a common criminal, a boastful blasphemer. But Jesus was the sinless Sovereign of the universe. He was no mere man, but was the magnificent Messiah. When they heard that message they cried out, "What must we do?"

13. Richard C. Trench, *Synonyms of the New Testament*, p. 258.

Peter responded, "Repent" (vv. 37-38). In this context, William Evans says that repentance means to change one's mind about Jesus Christ:

> Thus, when Peter, on the day of Pentecost, called upon the Jews to repent (Acts 2:14-40), he virtually called upon them to change their minds and their views regarding Christ. They had considered Christ to be a mere man, a blasphemer, an imposter. The events of the few preceding days had proven to them that He was none other than the righteous Son of God, their Savior and the Savior of the world. The result of their repentance or change of mind would be that they would receive Jesus Christ as their long promised Messiah.[14]

Still another object of repentance is works (see Heb. 6:1; Rev. 9:20; 16:11, etc.). As a general rule, mankind is of the opinion that works save. Oliver Wendell Holmes said, "To reach the port, we must sail, sometimes with the wind and sometimes against it, but we must sail and not drift, or lie at anchor."[15] Furthermore, modern man plays a game with his sin. Each individual is convinced that he is allowed a few miscues. The common concept is "If God grades on the curve, I'll make it." God declares that the works of man are unable to save. Our effort is dead works; it has no life or ability to rescue us. So men must repent of their dead works, that is, change their minds about their works.

Finally, the Scripture talks about repenting of sin (Rev. 9:21). Some sinners take a light view of sin. In their minds, sin is not serious. God's view is that sin is hideous. It separates humans from Himself. It causes destruction and death. To be saved, then, one must change his mind about his sin to see that it is his problem.

From this brief, simple study, it is obvious that repentance has several objects. In his book *What the Bible Teaches*, R.A. Torrey said, "What the repentance, or change of mind, is about must always be determined by the context."[16]

THE MARRIAGE OF REPENTANCE

In order to thoroughly understand repentance, we must understand its relationship to faith. Frankly, this is a puzzle and a problem.

14. William Evans, *Great Doctrines of the Bible*, p. 140.
15. Walter B. Knight, *Knight's Treasury of Illustrations*, p. 147.
16. Reuben A. Torrey, *What the Bible Teaches*, p. 355.

Sometimes repentance is the one and only stated requirement for salvation (Acts 17:30, 2 Pet. 3:9). In light of the New Testament doctrine of faith, repentance in these passages must include faith. After all, faith involves a change of mind from unbelief to belief (cf. Acts 11:17–18). Many times faith is the one and only requirement for salvation. That is the case in the gospel of John and in Romans 4. A few times, repentance and faith are listed together (Mark 1:15, Acts 20:21, Heb. 6:1). What is one to make of these statements? The conclusion seems to be that repentance and faith are not synonymous. When repentance occurs alone it includes faith. When faith occurs alone it implies repentance. Thus, they cannot be separated, but they ought to be distinguished. In salvation repentance is an inseparable part of, but is not synonymous with, faith.

Others have come to similar conclusions. Calvin said, "Can true repentance exist without faith? By no means. But although they cannot be separated, they ought to be distinguished."[17] Berkhoff put it this way:

> Moreover, true repentance never exists except in conjunction with faith, while, on the other hand, wherever there is true faith, there is also real repentance. The two are but different aspects of the same turning—a turning away from sin in the direction of God . . . . The two cannot be separated; they are simply complementary parts of the same process.[18]

Lewis Sperry Chafer concludes, "It [repentance] is included in believing and could not be separated from it [believing]."[19]

Repentance and faith are married. Like a husband and wife, they are one. They are Siamese twins who are born joined and cannot be separated. Spurgeon put it like this: "It is a great mystery; faith is before repentance in some of its aspects, and repentance before faith in another view of it; the fact being that they come into the soul together . . . . They are twins, and to say which is the elder born passes my knowledge."[20]

17. John Calvin, *Institutes of the Christian Religion*, p. 311.
18. Berkhoff, *Systematic Theology*, p. 487.
19. Chafer, *Systematic Theology*, 3:373.
20. Charles H. Spurgeon, "Faith and Repentance Inseparable," p. 402.

The wrong version of repentance goes like this: "You are a sinner. Be sorry for your sin. Stop sinning! Turn from your sin." The person who hears this will be convicted and will think he must change his life-style.

On the other hand, the correct view of repentance is more like this: "You are a sinner. You have the wrong view of God and Christ. You have sinned, and you cannot save yourself. Only Christ can help you. Throw yourself upon Him." The person who hears this will be convicted of his sin; but he will also be convinced that his works cannot save him, and he will come to Christ for salvation. God then changes the person inside, with a sometimes sudden and sometimes gradual change on the outside.

Donald Grey Barnhouse summed it up like this:

> The basic meaning of the original word, repentance, is 'to change one's mind,' and, since the idea of mental direction is involved, it is the equivalent to the military command 'about face!' Change of direction is involved in the process of becoming a Christian, but this must not be allowed to degenerate into the false idea of weeping for sin before salvation can be secured. (Soon after that, one would think that there must be further suffering for sins after death, and thus we would deny the finished work of Christ.) Biblical repentance may be described thus: the sinner has been trusting in himself for salvation, his back turned upon Christ, who is despised and rejected. Repent! About face! The sinner now despises and rejects himself, and places all confidence and trust in Christ. Sorrow for sin comes later, as the Christian grows in appreciation of the holiness of God, and the sinfulness of sin.[21]

---

21. Donald G. Barnhouse, *God's River*, 4:201-2.

11

What Is Faith?

I f there is anything that is clear in the New Testament, it is that a person is saved by faith. If there is anything that is unclear today, it is the nature of faith.

A college student once told me, "Faith is what you have to have when there is no evidence." Is faith a leap in the dark? Is it believing unsupported claims? Is faith a sophisticated synonym for superstition? Does faith begin where provable facts end?

I have had many men listen to me present the gospel only to tell me, "Oh, I believe it. I have faith." But then as I listen to them, all I hear is the chitter-chatter of men on a sinking ship who are trying to reassure one another that things will surely turn out all right. These people believe that someone, somewhere, sometime, somehow, will do something about the mess they are in. They have faith in faith.

It is vitally important that we understand faith. It is *the issue* in the New Testament. In John, the one book in the New Testament written to get people saved, the word "believe" *(pisteuō)* occurs ninety-nine times. The word "repent" *(metanoia)* does not occur once. Romans is the most detailed discussion of salvation in the New Testament, and obviously the issue is faith. The unmistakable point of Romans is that the believer, not the worker, is justified before God. Furthermore, in the Great Commission we are commanded to preach faith (cf. Mark 16:16). The word "gospel," both noun and verb, occurs 132 times in the New Testament. The word "repent," including the noun and verb, occurs only 58 times in the New Testament. But the word "faith," both its noun and verb forms, occurs 492 times. Obviously, the New Testament emphasizes faith.

What is faith? The Greek word has two basic elements: mental assent and reliance. These two elements assume a third, knowledge. Thus, faith consists of knowledge, mental assent, and reliance.

RECOGNITION OF TRUTH

Faith assumes knowledge, that is, recognition of some information. That is self-evident. Before we can believe anything, we must know about it. The Bible says, "How shall they believe in Him of whom they have not heard?"(Rom. 10:14). As though to emphasize this, the Bible sometimes puts hearing before believing. For example, Acts 18:8 says, "Many of the Corinthians, hearing, believed." Again, Ephesians 1:13 tells us, "In Him you also trusted, *after* you heard the word of truth, the gospel of your salvation" (italics added).

If faith presupposes knowledge, what does a person need to know? The object of faith in the New Testament is Jesus Christ. If you were to look up all the occurrences of "believe" and "faith" in the New Testament to see what a person must know about Christ, you would discover that a person must believe four things: (1) that Christ is God (John 20:31) and yet (2) a real man (1 John 4:2); (3) that He is the one who died for sins (Rom. 3:25) and (4) rose from the dead (Rom. 10:9).

In the New Testament those last two facts are called the gospel (1 Cor. 15:3–5). Mark says to preach the gospel, and the one who believes it will be saved. Peter says that the Gentiles heard of the gospel and believed (Acts 15:7). Paul says he is not ashamed of the gospel, for it is the power of God to salvation to everyone that believes (Rom. 1:16).

The object of faith is Jesus Christ, the God-Man, who died and arose. It is not just any "Christ."[1] The object of faith must be the Christ who is offered in the gospel, the one revealed in Scripture.

RECEPTION OF TRUTH

The second element of faith is mental assent. The knowledge

---

1. The Scripture warns that some may preach another Jesus (see Matt. 24:4,5; 2 Cor. 11:4).

received about Christ must now be accepted as true. The most basic meaning of *pisteuō* and *pistis,* the Greek words translated "believe" and "faith," is to "accept something as true," or be persuaded or convinced that something is true.

A person could have knowledge and not accept the information as true. In other words, he could not believe. A few years ago, the police in Phoenix, Arizona, found a three-year-old lad walking down the street. They figured he was big enough to at least partially identify himself. The desk sergeant kindly asked, "What is your name, sonny?"

"Baloney!" declared the youngster.

"Please," the sergeant pleaded, "tell me your real name."

"Baloney" was the reply. They tried bribes, but nothing worked. The mystery lad ate a candy bar and refused to change his story.

In the process of time, a lady called, voice quivering and filled with anxiety, to ask the police to help her find her lost son. Assuring her that he had already been found, the inquisitive officer asked, "What is his name, madam?"

"Baloney," replied the woman.

The police had knowledge, but they did not have mental assent. They did not accept the knowledge they had as true.

On the other hand, if there is both knowledge and acceptance, there is belief. For salvation, a person must know that Jesus Christ, the God-Man, died for sin and arose from the dead and accept that as factual and true.

Faith does not mean believing when there is no evidence; faith is believing the evidence. Faith is not built on ignorance, but on knowledge. Suppose a lawyer told two brothers that a distant relative from the old country had left them a large sum of money. The oldest accepted that information as factual, but the younger was skeptical. They both had knowledge. One *received* that knowledge, and the other did not. The one who had reception had faith. Notice carefully that believing you have inherited a million dollars when you haven't is not faith—it is sheer foolishness. Notice also that faith permits investigation. Faith is not having your feet planted in the mid-air of "I hope so." It is having your feet planted firmly on the ground of facts.

RELIANCE ON TRUTH

The third element of faith is trust. *pisteuō* and *pistis* ("believe" and "faith") refer to resting in, relying on, or depending upon something or someone. Often the New Testament emphasizes this and makes it even stronger by adding a preposition after "believe." For example, John 3:36 says, "He who believes *in* the Son has everlasting life," and Acts 16:31 says, "Believe *on* the Lord Jesus Christ, and you will be saved" (italics added).

A truck driver may believe the bridge is safe, but he does not believe in the biblical sense until he drives onto the bridge. A person may believe the elevator will carry him to the top of the building, but he does not believe in the New Testament sense until he steps into it. A person with his clothes on fire may believe that the swimming pool will save him, but he is not saved until he dives into the pool. Faith is acceptance plus reliance.

Simply to know about Christ will not save. To accept as true the facts about Him will not save. Even to acknowledge that Christ actually died for sin and literally rose from the dead will not save. One must believe *on* Christ, that is, depend on Him, trust Him. Saving faith is not believing a proposition; it is trusting a person. Only when a person trusts Christ, depends on Him who died and arose, is he saved.

Faith is accepting something as true and depending on that something. This assumes knowledge. Thus, faith is the recognition of truth, the reception of truth, and the reliance upon truth.

Charles Hodge, the famous nineteenth-century Princeton theologian, says:

> That faith, therefore, which is connected with salvation, includes knowledge, that is, a perception of the truth and its qualities; assent, or the persuasion of truth of the object of faith; and trust, or reliance. The exercise, or state of mind expressed by the word faith, as used in the Scriptures, is not mere mental assent, or mere trust, it is the intelligent perception, reception, and reliance on the truth as revealed in the gospel.[2]

THE OBJECT OF FAITH

Faith does not save. Faith is not magic; there is no saving virtue in it. Christ saves.

Faith is merely the means by which the benefits of Christ's death

2.   Charles Hodge, *Commentary on the Epistle to the Romans,* p. 29

are applied to the individual. The New Testament does not teach that a person is saved on account of his faith, but rather, that he is saved through faith. The saving power resides not in the act of faith, nor in the nature of faith, but exclusively in the object of faith—Christ. J. Gresham Machen in his book *What Is Faith?* puts it like this: "The New Testament never says that a man is saved *on account of* his faith, but always that he is saved *through* his faith, or *by means of* his faith; faith is merely the means which the Holy Spirit uses to apply to the individual soul the benefits of Christ's death."[3]

All that is needed is a little faith. Jesus said an amount the size of a mustard seed would do (Luke 17:6). A mustard seed is tiny. The issue, then, is not the amount, but the object of faith. The question is whether the object of faith is able to do the job. A great amount of faith in a bridge too weak to support you would do you no good, but a small amount of faith in a bridge that would support you—just enough to get you on it—is enough to get you across it.

Imagine a ship filled with peeople crossing the Atlantic. In the middle of the ocean there is an explosion. The ship is severely damaged and slowly sinking. Most are dead, and the rest are rushing for the lifeboats. Now suppose one man doesn't know about the lifeboat, so he does not get aboard. He doesn't have knowledge, so he is not saved. Suppose another man knows about the lifeboat and believes it will save his life, but he is grief-stricken over seeing his wife killed, so he chooses not to get aboard and dies with his wife. He has knowledge and mental assent, but he is not saved. Others believe the lifeboat will save them, and they get into the boat. They are saved by faith, that is, they have knowledge, mental assent, and trust. However, it is not their f aith that saves them—no matter how much they have. It is the boat. Saving faith trusts Christ, and Christ saves.

3. J. Gresham Machen, *What Is Faith?* p. 180.

12

Don't Ask Jesus to Come into Your Heart

Shortly after I was saved, an experienced soul-winner taught me how to lead people to Christ. He gave me a booklet that told me everything. It told me what verses to use and what to say. As my tutor handed me the booklet he said,, "This will tell you everything you need to know, but there is just one thing missing. The author's presentation includes everything but the gospel."

Imagine a booklet on how to lead someone to Christ containing everything but the gospel. Sure enough, the recommended verses to be used were Romans 3:23, Romans 6:23, John 1:12, and Revelation 3:20. The problem was easily corrected. My mentor suggested I insert Romans 5:8 after Romans 6:23.

So, armed with a practical presentation of God's dynamite, I marched into life to capture people for Christ, and I did. For the next several years I led several hundred people to the Lord. In the process, I came to believe that there was another problem with the presentation given in that booklet. It all began when I started to teach others how to lead people to Christ. I was still in college at the time, but I trained other students and took them out to witness.

One day I watched one of those trainees talk to a teenage fellow. As I listened, it was evident the teenager did not understand what he was doing and did not get saved. Yet when the counselor was done, the young man believed that he was saved. That high school student had no conviction of sin, no conception of Christ's dying in his place to pay for his sin, no comprehension of trusting in Christ alone for salvation. Rather, just about all he got was that he was to bow his head and ask Jesus into his heart.

After he did that to get the counselor off his back, he was asked, "Do you know for sure that you are saved?"

He answered, "No!"

Then the counselor (mind you, the one I trained), instead of going back to the basics of sin, the cross, and faith, tried to convince the fellow he was saved because he had prayed a prayer. "After all," he argued, "you asked Jesus to come into your heart, and He said He would, didn't He?" Who could possibly answer that?

That day, I doubted. I doubted that asking Jesus to come into your heart was valid. That provoked me to study. Since then I have come to the conclusion that the Bible does not teach that a person gets saved by asking Jesus Christ to come into his heart or into his life.

THE BIBLE SAYS A SINNER MUST "BELIEVE"

In the first place, the biblical expression for what a sinner must do is "believe." God could have used any word He wished. He could have set it in any language. He could have created a word or a whole language. But He chose *pisteuō*, "believe," and *pistis*, "faith," and he used them emphatically. In John, the one New Testament book written to get people saved, *pisteuō* occurs ninety-nine times (while *metauoeō*, "repent," does not occur once). Furthermore, in Paul's most extended theological discourse on salvation, the book of Romans, he used one word, "faith." In Romans, one whole chapter (chap. 4) is given to that subject. There are other words used for what a sinner must do to be saved. "Look," "come," and others are employed, but these are used as synonyms for faith.

Sometimes it is objected that people do not understand what it is to "believe." If that is the case, then they are simply not ready to be saved. In Matthew 13:13–16 Jesus taught that if people did not understand, they could not be saved. He even spoke in parables so they would not understand.

NO PASSAGE TEACHES THAT A SINNER IS SAVED
BY ASKING JESUS INTO HIS HEART

"BEHOLD, I STAND AT THE DOOR"

In the second place, no passage states, or even implies that a sinner is saved by asking Jesus to come into his heart. The one most commonly used to suggest that it does is Revelation 3:20. But that passage does not teach that one is to ask Jesus to come into his heart to be saved.

The context of Revelation 3:20 is the Lord's letter to Laodicea. In verses 15-17 the Lord talks about their condition. In verses 18-20 He offers His counsel. In describing their condition the Lord says He knows their works (vv. 15-16), their words (v. 17*a*), and who they are (v. 17*b*). He calls them "lukewarm." Note carefully that the subject here is not salvation, but works, or service. The Laodiceans were half-hearted in their service. The Lord says, "I could wish you were cold [and know your need], or hot [and have no need]." But instead, they were lukewarm. They had just enough to satisfy themselves, but not enough to be completely committed and satisfy God. Hot tea is usable, and iced tea is also usable, but lukewarm tea you spit out. So when He tasted of their works, it made Him want to vomit. To be half-hearted in service results in being a castaway (cf. 1 Cor. 9:24-27).

The Lord goes on to describe their pride. Laodicea was one of the wealthiest cities in the world. This material wealth produced an independent, self-sufficient attitude in the people of the city. They thought they had need of nothing. In AD 61 an earthquake devastated the city. The Roman government offered to help them rebuild, but the people were so proud they refused and rebuilt the city using their own resources. The attitude in the city was absorbed by the church. The citizens said, "We don't need government," and the Christians said, "We don't need God." Make no mistake: material wealth can cause a Christian to be self-sufficient and not dependent on the Lord (cf. 1 Tim. 6:17).

After examining their works and their words the Lord evaluates what they are. His conclusion is that they are in dire spiritual need and don't even know it. His assessment is expressed in terms with which they could immediately identify. Laodiceans were rich; He tells them they are poor. Laodicea had a world-famous medical center that was particularly known for treating eye disease; He informs them that they are blind. Laodicea was a center for manufacturing clothing; He declares that they are naked. The point is, of course, that they were deceived concerning their spiritual condition. Obviously, an unbeliever can be deceived about his spiritual condition and be described as poor and blind; but so can a Christian. The New Testament clearly indicates that a Christian can be deceived about his spiritual condition (James 1:22), and be poor (1 Tim. 6:18), and blind (2 Pet. 1:9).

Having summarized their condition, the Lord offers some counsel. He tells them they need to be faithful (v. 18). They need to be faithful to the Lord so that they might have faith tested by fire, personal righteousness, and vision. They also need to be fervent (v. 19). *paidenō* ("chasten") refers to child training, the activity of God to believers (Heb. 12:5–8, especially v. 8). Furthermore, they are to be zealous. And one other piece of advice: they need fellowship. That is the point of verse 20: if a Christian invites Christ to dinner, He will come, and they will have fellowship together.

But before considering verse 20, note carefully that the context of this passage is a letter to believers. The passage is addressed to the Laodicean *church*. Granted, these people are half-hearted, self-sufficient, and deceived about their spiritual need; but they are believers. The crowning indication of that is that the Lord tells them in verse 19 that He will chasten them.

Now, verse 20 itself says Christ will come "in to" (two different words), not come "into" (one word). The verse is saying that Christ will come *in* the church *to* the person, not that Christ will come *into* the person. When He gets in the church with the person He will eat dinner with him. That is, He will have fellowship with him.

This is not a hair-splitting of the English text, but an accurate reflection of the Greek. In Greek, "come in" (*eiserchomai*) is one word. It is followed by the preposition "to" (*pros*). That construction occurs eight times in the New Testament (Mark 6:25, 15:43; Luke 1:28; Acts 10:3, 11:3, 17:2, 28:8; Rev. 3:20). In each instance it means to enter into a building and stand before a person.

If Jesus had meant that He would enter into the person, there is another construction He could have used. That is the word "come in" (*eiserchomai*) plus the preposition "into" (*eis*). That combination is used 136 times in the New Testament for entrance into a building, a city, a closet, and even a person. As a matter of fact, every time "come into" is used of entrance into a person it is followed by the preposition *eis*. There are only four such cases in the New Testament (Mark 9:25; Luke 8:30; 22:3; John 13:27), and every one refers to demon possession. Therefore, the "come in to" of Revelation 3:20 means entrance into a building in order to meet a person. If entrance into a person were meant, another Greek construction would have been used.

This conclusion is confirmed by the Arndt and Gingrich *Lexicon*. The authors list one possible meaning of *eiserchomai* as "enter into someone." They list another possibility as "to come or go *to* someone." Under this latter one, they list Revelation 3:20.[1] In commenting on the use of the two Greek prepositions in question, C.F.D. Moule says, "It may be added, as a rough-and-ready distinction between the meaning of eis and pros, that eis tends to include the idea of *entry*, whereas pros tends to stop short at going *up to* (without entering)."[2]

The point of Revelation 3:20 is that those lukewarm, self-sufficient, spiritually deceived believers had pushed God aside; and they needed fellowship and faithfulness. It is not teaching that a person is saved by asking Jesus into his heart. It is not even talking about salvation!

"AS MANY AS RECEIVED HIM"

Another verse often used to support "asking Jesus to come into your heart" is John 1:12. But that verse is not teaching that a person should ask Jesus to come into his heart or his life to do anything. A careful study of this passage will indicate that.

First, look at the context. In verse 10, John declares that Jesus came to the world. But the world did not recognize Him. They did not even know He was here. Think of it: He who made the world was in the world, and the world didn't even know it. At the time, the center of the world was Rome. All roads led there. Jesus walked and wandered around the dusty roads of obscure Galilee. Who ever heard—who ever cared—about Galilee? Literally, He was in the world He made, and it did not know He was there.

1. W. F. Arndt and F. W. Gingrich, *A Greek-English Lexicon of the New Testament and Other Early Christian Literature*, p. 232.
2. C.F.D. Moule, *An Idiom Book of New Testament Greek*, pp. 67-68.

John next considers Israel. In verse 11 we are told He came to His own, that is, His own people Israel, and they did not welcome Him. Unlike the world, they at least knew He was there; but like the world, they didn't care. John says they did not welcome Him. They crucified Him. With a brief stroke of the pen, John has dismissed the world and Israel. Now, in verse 12, He drops down to individuals. The first word of verse 12 is "but" (*de*), a word of contrast. In contrast to the world and Israel, only individuals who "receive" (*lambanō*) Christ will become sons of God.

What is meant by "receive"? A subjective receiving of Christ into your heart or life? No. The "but" demands that this receiving is in contrast to the world and Israel. John is simply saying that in contrast to the world and Israel, if any individual does *recognize* and *welcome* Christ, he will become a child of God. Dean Henry Alford, the famous Greek exegete, says that "receive" here means some "recognized Him as that which He was—the Word of God and Light of men."[3] Alfred Plummer says it "denotes the spontaneous acceptance of the Messiah."[4]

The pertinent question is, How does one receive Him? By asking Him in? Again, the answer is no. John explains at the end of verse 12—"even to those who believe in His name." F. L. Godet, who wrote one of the classic commentaries on John, put it like this: "The figurative, and consequently, somewhat vague, term *receive*, required to be explained, precisely defined; for the readers must know accurately the means by which they may place themselves among the number of 'all those who.' Hence the apprehended phrase . . . 'to those who believe in His name.' "[5]

In other words, John 1:12 is not teaching that a sinner is to ask Jesus to come into his heart. It is telling us to accept Christ for who He is, and that acceptance is trusting Him as Savior.

"WHOEVER CALLS UPON THE NAME OF THE LORD"

Still another verse that has been used to support the idea of asking Jesus to come into one's heart is Romans 10:13. The question is, What is the content of the calling? Or, What is said when one calls on the name of the Lord? Verse 9 says, "Confess with your

3. Dean Henry Alford, *The Greek New Testament*, 1:684.
4. Alfred Plummer, *The Gospel According to St. John*, p. 66.
5. F. L. Godet, *Commentary on the Gospel of John*, 1:265.

mouth the Lord Jesus." *Homologeō*, "confess," literally means to say the same thing, to agree, to acknowledge. God says that Jesus Christ is His Son, that Jesus Christ died for sin, and that Jesus Christ arose from the dead. To confess Jesus Christ is to agree with God, to say those same things about Christ that God does.

Actually, various explanations of the call have been suggested. William G.T. Shedd has said, "Prayer to Christ for mercy and salvation is an act in which faith in Christ shows itself."[6] Charles Ryrie contends that "Lord," or "Jehovah," is the Old Testament name for God; and thus he who confesses that Jesus is Lord affirms His Diety.[7] The one thing that is clear is that there is no hint in the passage that one is to ask Jesus to come into his heart.

BIBLICAL EVANGELISM

By this time, the conclusion is obvious. The biblical expression for what a sinner must do to be saved is "believe," not ask Jesus to come into his heart. But to crystalize and clarify that even more, several observations need to be made.

First of all, people have been saved when a wrong verse or model has been used. I am not saying, nor have I ever said, that people have not been saved when Revelation 3:20 was used. On the contrary, I do think that people have been saved when this verse was used, but in my opinion that was in spite of the verse and not because of it. Augustine was saved when he read Romans 13:14. Does that mean we should use Romans 13:14 to lead a person to Christ? I once met a lady who swore that when she was saved she didn't know anything else to do, so she prayed the Lord's prayer. Does that mean the Lord's prayer should be used to lead someone to Christ? There are people who have heard and understood the gospel that have not trusted Christ. They are confronted again, and this time decide to come to Christ. They use the "ask Jesus to come in" prayer. In their case, they understood all the right things, and the words were almost immaterial.

On the other hand, people have been deceived by this approach. I am personally convinced that many who have prayed asking Jesus to come into their hearts were not really regenerated. But because

6. William G.T. Shedd, *A Critical and Doctrinal Commentary of the Epistle of St. Paul to the Romans*, p. 231.
7. Charles C. Ryrie, *Balancing the Christian Life*, pp. 173–76.

they were told that praying that prayer was the means of salvation, they thought they were saved. How much better it would be to point people to Christ and the cross and exhort them to trust Him and His finished work.

Once a pastor and I were talking to a lady who said she was saved. The pastor asked her what she did to get saved, and she replied, "I asked Jesus to come into my heart." Not satisfied with that, he asked, "If you were to stand before God and God were to ask, 'Why should I let you into My heaven,' what would you say?" Her response was, "I love God and I deserve it." The more we talked, the more obvious it became that she had no comprehension of salvation and no relationship with Jesus Christ; but she thought she was saved because she had asked Jesus to come into her heart.

Let me state the whole issue another way. Biblically, faith is the *means* of salvation. The indwelling of Christ is the *result*. There are other results of salvation. Take, for example, the sealing of the Holy Spirit. It is no more proper to make His indwelling (that is, asking Jesus to come into your heart) the means than it is to make sealing the means. If you told someone to pray to ask God to seal him with the Spirit, and the person did, would that person be saved? My personal opinion is that we cannot really say one way or the other. It depends on whether or not that person understood the gospel and trusted Christ. We must be biblical, and the biblical word for what a person must do to be saved is "believe."

Part 4

The Principles of Evangelism

13

Who Did It?

Let me introduce the characters and plot; then you decide.

Mr. and Mrs. Smith had a son named Joe. Immediately, a godly grandmother began to pray. She pleaded with God to save Joe and use him. Mr. and Mrs. Smith were also concerned. They, too, prayed. They lived godly, Christian lives before him. They took him to church. Then there was Aunt Martha. She was not Joe's aunt; that was her nickname—all the children at church called her that. She was a talented teacher who faithfully taught Bible stories in a captivating way. And, oh, yes, there was Pastor Pritchard. He preached and Joe listened—sometimes.

Then one day an evangelist came to speak at Joe's church. He was energetic and dynamic. Joe was moved. He, and a number of others, went to the front at the end of the message. There a counselor explained the gospel to Joe, and he trusted Christ.

Who led Joe to Christ? The counselor . . . the evangelist . . . the pastor . . . Aunt Martha . . . Father and Mother . . . Grandma Smith . . . God?

As for a complicated crime, a number of cases could be constructed. In one sense, the counselor did it; yet without the evangelist he could not have. You can believe the evangelist added Joe to *his* total, and told the story as if he did it. The pastor at least had a part. So did Aunt Martha, the parents, and Grandma Smith. A Calvinist would argue that God did it.

Well, who really did it?

GOD IS SEEKING AND SAVING SINNERS

To answer that question we need to know several pertinent spiritual truths. To begin, we need to know that God seeks men (Luke 19:10). The story of Zacchaeus illustrates that well. He was a rich tax-collector with a bad reputation. Other than his effort to see Jesus out of curiosity, there is no indication he was seeking for the Savior or for salvation. It was Jesus who was seeking him.

That is the way it has always been. When Adam sinned there was no indication that he began to search and seek out God. He and Eve were too busy covering their nakedness. When God did initiate the process, they did not run to Him, they ran from Him. Genesis 3:8 says they hid themselves! They did not seek God; God sought them.

That is the way it is today. According to Ephesians 2, men are spiritually dead. They are not just bad, they are dead. They are blind. They do not need glasses; they need eyes. They do not seek God (Rom. 3:11; 1 Cor. 1:23; 2:14).

Theologians teach that men are not seeking God; evangelists preach that men are. The theologians read their Bibles and conclude that men are not interested in finding God. Evangelists meet men who seem to be trying to find God, and conclude that men are seeking God. Who is right? Both. It is because of God's work that some begin to search.

Some years ago a five-year-old boy became lost in the Northwest. As night grew near the family grew frantic with anxiety. Sympathetically, many others joined in searching for the missing lad. Snow began to fall, hindering the efforts. Despite their valiant endeavors, the little boy could not be found. The next morning the weary father, having looked all night, decided to return home for a short rest. A half mile from the house he kicked against what seemed to be a log lying across the pathway. Suddenly the snow-covered bundle moved, and a small boy stretched, yawned, sat up, and exclaimed, "Oh, Daddy! I found you at last!" The father was overjoyed that the child, although badly frost-bitten, was still alive; the boy thought he had found the father.

Because God is working in the world, some are ready to be saved. To the theologically untrained or biblically unaware evangelists who meet a number of people God has prepared, it appears that these people are "hungry for the gospel." And they are! In John 4 Jesus tells us that there are more prepared people than we think. The fields are white, ready for harvest. Because God is working in the world, some are ready to be saved.

God is not only seeking. He is saving sinners. The whole Trinity is involved in saving a person. The Father planned it, the Son provided it, and the Holy Spirit produces it. The Trinitarian involvement in salvation is clearly spelled out in Ephesians 1. In Ephesians 1:3–6, Paul tells us of the work of God the Father. He has chosen us, adopted us, and accepted us. In verses 7–12 the work of the Son is revealed. He has redeemed us, forgiven us, revealed God's will to us, and made us an inheritance. In verses 13–14 we are told of the work of the Holy Spirit. He has sealed us and given us a pledge. In Titus 3:4–7 Paul calls God our Savior. He then talks about the part that God the Father had, the portion of God the Spirit, and the part of God the Son. Biblical evangelism is Trinitarian.

But if God does all the work, then why not just let Him do it, and we do nothing? To answer that, as well as the other questions at the beginning of this chapter, we must note a second spiritual truth.

GOD USES MEN TO REACH MEN

In Romans 10:14 Paul boldly declares that people cannot hear and believe without a preacher. In his comment on this verse, Dean Henry Alford said, "The apostle is showing the *necessity* and the *dignity* of the preacher of the word."[1] George W. Peters has put it like this: "God has chosen human instruments to accomplish His task in human hearts within a human society surrounded by human environment."[2] God's method is men. We are looking for methods, but God is looking for men.

To emphasize the fact that God uses men, let us look at the other possibilities. God could save men directly, that is, apart from any means. As a matter of fact, He did just that in the Garden of Eden. After Adam sinned he sewed fig leaves to cover himself and sat where he thought God could not see him, and God personally came to reestablish the broken relationship. The objection could be raised that Adam was the first man. There were no other men to send to him. True, but the point is that God could have, and did, save Adam and Eve directly, apart from any other means. If that instance is not enough, consider Acts 9. The Lord saved Paul directly, apart from any

---

1. Dean Henry Alford, *The Greek New Testament,* 2:421.
2. George W. Peters, *A Biblical Theology of Missions,* p. 163.

preacher or pastor. He personally spoke, and Paul was immediately converted on the spot. Let's face it: God could do the job Himself by personally appearing and speaking. Instead, He chooses to use men.

Or, consider that God could use animals. He did once. In Numbers 22:28 God used a donkey to speak to Balaam. If Walt Disney can put words in the mouth of a duck, God can put a message in the mouth of a donkey. God could use angels. That is not as farfetched as you might think. God has used angels to deliver messages (e.g., Dan. 10:1-9). More important, He used angels to inform the shepherds of the birth of Christ (Luke 2:7-14). Furthermore, they announced that the Babe was the Savior, and Luke uses the word "evangelize" *(euangelizomai)* to describe what they did (Luke 2:10). Paul entertained the possibility of angels preaching the gospel (Gal. 1:8). Angelic evangelists may be theoretical now, but that will be a reality in the Tribulation Period (see Rev. 14:6). D.L. Moody once said in a sermon,

> I believe that if an angel were to wing his way from earth up to heaven, and were to say that there was one poor, ragged boy without father or mother to care for him, teach him the way of life, and if God were to ask who among them were willing to come down to earth and live there for fifty years and lead that one to Jesus Christ, every angel in heaven would volunteer to go. Even Gabriel, who stands in the presence of the Almightly would say, "Let me leave my high and lofty position, and let me have the luxury of leading one soul to Christ." There is no greater honor than to be the instrument of God's hand of leading one person out of the kingdom of Satan into the glorious light of heaven.[3]

God seeks to save, but God uses men to do the job. In the two thousand years since Christ was physically here, men have developed many means of communication: the printing press, the radio, the telephone, the television. All of these have been pressed into evangelistic service. God has been pleased to use them to bring millions to Himself, but even here God's method is people. Men must write. Men must speak. Men must run the presses and the TV stations. God employs men.

If we in the church are to win people to Christ, we are going to have to get personally involved. We can put ads in the paper, spots

3. This quote, evidently from one of Moody's sermons, found its way into my sermon illustration file. Unfortunately, I have no documentation.

on the radio, and letters in the mail; but that is no substitute for personal contact, personal presentation, and personal invitation to trust Christ.

God uses men and wants to use you. At the beginning of this chapter I asked, Who did it? The answer is, All of them. Or more accurately, God did it and used all of them. A fable illustrates this truth well. According to this myth, when Jesus ascended and arrived back in heaven he was met by Gabriel who asked, "Did You die?" Of course, the Lord responded in the affirmative. Gabriel said, "Now the whole world knows, right?" The Lord had to tell him no. Gabriel, shocked, blurted out, "Well, do You have a plan?" The Lord nodded yes. "What is it," inquired Gabriel. "Peter," said the Lord. "Peter!" exclaimed Gabriel, disturbed and upset, "He's the fickle fellow who denied You. What if he fails? What's Plan B?" The Lord responded, "My plan is Peter; there is no plan B."

14

The Gift of Evangelism

The Bible clearly teaches that there is a gift of evangelism, but that is where the clarity stops. What is involved in the gift of evangelism? Lewis Sperry Chafer defined an evangelist as "a pioneer missionary to the hitherto unevangelized."[1] John F. Walvoord has stated that the gift of evangelism is the "unusual capacity to preach the gospel of salvation and to win the lost to Christ."[2] A Bible teacher once suggested that it is the ability to make the gospel clear. Yet another teacher contends that it is the ability to get results and teach witnessing. One professor even suggested that it is the ability to think like a lost man.[3]

DEFINITION OF THE GIFT

The gift of evangelism is the special ability—the God-given spiritual talent—to communicate the gospel to sinners. That is evident from *euangelistēs*, "evangelist," which literally means "one who announces the gospel." It is used three times in the New Testament. In Ephesians 4:11–12 Paul says that God gives men who are gifted as evangelists to the church. Philip the deacon is

---

1. Lewis Sperry Chafer, *True Evangelism*, p. 6.
2. John F. Walvoord, *The Holy Spirit at Work Today*, p. 40.
3. These comments were related to me in private conversations with, respectively, Dr. Dwight Pentecost, Dr. Stanley Toussaint, and Dr. Haddon Robinson.

called an evangelist in Acts 21:8. Timothy is urged to do the work of an evangelist in 2 Timothy 4:5.

In his book *Evangelism*, G. Campbell Morgan explains:

> A man who receives the gift of evangelist is one to whom there is given a clear understanding of the evangel, a great passion in his heart results from the clear vision, a great optimism fills his soul, born of his confidence in the power of Christ to save every man; and growing out of that passion and that confidence a great constraint seizes him to tell somebody, to tell everybody the glad news of salvation by Jesus Christ.[4]

In other words, an evangelist tells people the good news. It is unfortunate that many evangelists major in bad news.

But the gift of evangelism also includes the special ability to equip saints. Ephesians 4:12 indicates that. Jack Arnold clarifies: "The term evangelist, in its primary sense, is a person sovereignly endowed with the gift of evangelism, who has, as his primary purpose, the evangelizing of the lost, and also has as his secondary responsibility the equipping of the saints for evangelism."[5]

The gift of evangelism, then, is the special ability to communicate the gospel to sinners and equip saints to evangelize. That definition implies several things.

For one thing, an evangelist is able to communicate to non-Christians, which means he can think like a nonbeliever. After a lapse of time, a degree of spiritual growth, and extended exposure to the Christian community, many saints forget what it is like to live in the world, totally apart from God. It is like being married for years and forgetting what it is like to be single. An evangelist seems to have a native ability to understand where the non-Christian is "coming from." Thus, he can identify with him and communicate to him.

An evangelist may also have a special ability to reap. Dr. Lee Roberson of Tennessee Temple University, would on occasion take Dr. John McCormick, then a Bible teacher at his school, with him to speak in churches. After several years of that kind of activity, McCormick said, "I could speak on salvation and nothing would happen. He could speak on anything and people would get saved."

---

4. G. Campbell Morgan, *Evangelism*, p. 55.
5. Jack Arnold, "Principles of Evangelism in the Book of Acts," p. 4.

If an evangelist has a gift to equip saints, he probably has some ability to teach. At least he will be a communicator. When he ministers, saints will learn not only information but skill in approaching a sinner.

An evangelist will probably be able to motivate. If he doesn't turn people off at first with his enthusiasm, he will turn them on.

All of this does not mean that an evangelist has a special kind of personality. He is not necessarily an extrovert. I have known introverts with the gift of evangelism, but at the same time I would also have to say that although an evangelist may not be an extrovert, every evangelist I have known has been an incurable optimist.

An evangelist does not necessarily dress a certain way. There is no such thing as an evangelist costume. In the south, evangelists have often worn white shoes, red ties, and flashy clothes. That is part of the culture, not part of the gift. Yet an evangelist knows, by his gift, that clothes either help or hinder him in evangelism, since he understands non-Christians and communication. He knows that clothes communicate. Consequently he will probably dress either to get attention or to identify with his audience.

DESCRIPTION OF THE GIFT

From experience I have concluded that the gift of evangelism exists in different shapes and sizes.

For example, there is a gift that specializes in personal evangelism. The person with this gift is successful in personal evangelism but not in public meetings. A pastor I know has led many to Christ personally. Consequently, he was invited on many occasions to conduct evangelistic crusades. By his own admission, he was a failure in the mass meetings and finally came to the conclusion he should refuse to conduct evangelistic crusades, though he remained highly successful in personal evangelism.

On the other hand, a person may have the gift that manifests itself in public evangelism. One would think that an evangelist who had an ability to evangelize publicly would be successful in personal soul-winning. However, that is not always the case. I know of one evangelist who has been highly successful in pulpit evangelism for many years, and yet he has confessed poor success in leading people to Christ privately, though he has tried.

Some with the gift seem to specialize in training believers to be evangelists. Bill Bright and James Kennedy are outstanding examples of this. Each has manifested his gift of evangelism in equipping saints.

Women can have the gift of evangelism. Philippians 4:3 seems to indicate that. A Christian housewife once said to me, "What's wrong with me? I'd rather be with sinners than with saints." A few questions revealed that she was not "worldly"; she was just interested in reaching the world with the gospel. Her gift naturally pushed her in that direction.

There is also the possibility of combining the spiritual gift with the natural talent. Some gifted evangelists have combined their talent for writing with their gift of evangelism and have won hundreds and thousands to Christ through literature. Do not some evangelists combine their gift for winning the lost with their talent for singing? The point is that the gift of evangelism includes various types.

DEPLOYMENT OF THE GIFT

Some people get the idea that the possession of the gift automatically guarantees success in reaping. They think that if they can get an evangelist to talk to their friend, or get him to hear an evangelist, he will be saved. But there is more to successful reaping than being a gifted farmer.

Paul exhorted Timothy to "stir up" his gift (2 Tim. 1:6). The Greek word means "rekindle," or keep in full flame. Imagine the fire in a fireplace burning low. The coals need to be stirred up. New logs must be tossed on the fire. Likewise, a gift-possessor may need to stir up his fire. This includes using his gift and perhaps developing his gift by watching and listening to others with the same gift. By practice and use, a person perfects his ability. A teenager may be a gifted pianist and still need to stir up his talent. Older performers, even those not as gifted as the youngster, may still be able to teach the younger player many things. Remember, being a talented farmer does not guarantee a bumper crop.

Successful reaping also depends on circumstances. Jesus, God in the flesh, could not do mighty works in His hometown because of the residents' unbelief (Mark 6:1-6). When the nation rejected Him, He told the parable of the sower. The problem was not the sower, nor the seed, nor the sowing, but the soil. Billy Graham would not be as successful in a Moslem country as he has been in America. For great success, there must be good soil.

To sum up, the gift of evangelism consists fundamentally of a special spiritual ability to communicate the gospel to sinners and to equip saints for evangelism. There are different manifestations of the gift, but all forms must be exercised and developed to have the greatest possible success.

There are two practical applications of this biblical truth. In the first place, we need to use not only gifted evangelists; the church needs to be exposed to all the gifts, especially the ministering gifts. When a church is exposed to one gift only, believers become lopsided and unbalanced. If all they hear is a teacher, they end up spiritually fat. If all they get is exhortation, they end up lean and mean. So every church needs to be exposed to a variety of gifts, so that it can be balanced and blessed.

Second, we must all learn from the gifted saints among us. Some Christians have used the existence of gifts as an excuse not to be involved. That is to misunderstand the nature and purpose of gifts. God has given to some special ability and to all responsibility. God has given every believer many responsiblilities, including evangelism, exhortation, teaching, giving, and showing mercy. Then, God has given some special abilities, or gifts, in these areas. I believe God gave spiritual gifts to individuals so that they could teach other believers their area of responsibility. That is the point of Ephesians 4.

For example, God has given all believers the responsibility of giving. He has also given some believers the special ability (that is, the gift) of giving. I have given money to the Lord all of my Christian life, but I must say frankly that I did not know how to give until I met a man who had the gift. My exposure to him and my experience with him taught me more about giving than everything else put together. But suppose I had said, "I don't have to give because I don't have the gift." You see, you may not have special *ability*, but you do have *responsibility* to give money—and to give the message of salvation.

15

The Man God Uses

God's method is men, but what kind of man does God use? What type of person does God desire to use? All agree God wants His servants to be spiritual and to be evangelistic. There is even a general consensus that there is a relationship between the two; but that is where the agreement ends. What does it mean to be spiritual? What is being evangelistic? It is not surprising that there is no agreement on the relationship between the two.

Some teach a passive view of spirituality. "Let go and let God" is their slogan. Others preach an active view of spirituality. Their cry is "Get going and let God."

What does it mean to be evangelistic? Is it witnessing with your walk, or winning with your talk? A friend of mine attempts to witness to every person he meets. If he does not talk to them about Christ, which he usually does, he gives them a tract. Another friend argues that we must love people into the kingdom of God.

What is spirituality? What is being evangelistic? What is the relationship between the two?

THE SPIRITUAL LIFE

The spiritual life is first and foremost a life of faith. "The just shall live by faith," (Heb. 10:38); this is true of both salvation and sanctification. In Galatians 2:20 Pauls says, "the life which I now live in the flesh I live by faith in the Son of God." The Christian Hall of Fame is a hall of fame of faith. Hebrews 11 repeats over and over the expression "by faith . . ." The life of faith believes God's Word and trusts God's Person. Faith hears from God's Word and accepts as true God's point of view. Faith depends upon God's grace and power for the ability to do what God says.

The spiritual life also includes obedience. In Matthew 4:19 Jesus told the disciples, "Follow Me," meaning "imitate Me, obey Me." Later, as recorded in John 14:15, He said, "If you love Me, keep My commandments." One of Paul's favorite expressions for the Christian life is "walk" (*peripateō*). He exhorts believers to walk as children of light. Charles Ryrie says, "To walk in the light [1 John 1:7] is to live in obedience to God's commandments."[1] James sums it up in James 1:22 when he says, "Be doers of the word." The spiritual life, then, is a life of effort. Galatians 5:16 does not say to sit in the Spirit; it says to walk in the Spirit.

The songwriter struck the proper balance when he said, "Trust and obey, for there's no other way to be happy in Jesus, but to trust and obey." In the debate between passivity and activity in the spiritual life, it is not either/or, it is both/and. There is a sense in which we let go and let God. We rest in Him. But we must also get going and let God. We do not just rest.

EVANGELISM IS A RESULT OF THE SPIRITUAL LIFE

There are many results of the spiritual life. The greatest is love. Another is evangelism. Jesus said, "Come after Me, and I will make you become fishers of men" (Mark 1:17). In Acts 1:8 He says, "You shall receive power when the Holy Spirit has come upon you; and you shall be witnesses to Me." Peter urges, "Sanctify the Lord God in your hearts, and always be ready to give a defense to everyone who asks you a reason for the hope that is in you, with meekness and fear" (1 Pet. 3:15). The spiritual life comes before and produces evangelism. Following precedes fishing, power precedes proclamation.

If the spiritual life is a life of faith and obedience, then evangelism is the result of the spiritual life. God commands us to "go into all the world and preach the gospel to every creature" (Mark 16:15).

---

1. *The Ryrie Study Bible*, King James Version, p. 1771.

Do we believe? Do we obey? If the result of the spiritual life is conformity to Christ, then evangelism is the result of the spiritual life. Jesus came "to seek and to save that which was lost" (Luke 19:10). If we are to be conformed to the Shepherd, then we will seek lost sheep. If we value what God values, we will value men and their salvation. If we desire what God desires, we will long to see people saved. If we walk with Him, we will run after those who are going astray.

That does not mean that the result will be spontaneous, though many have taught that it will be. It has been said that the New Testament has a remarkable absence of the command to witness. I don't think it ever occurred to the early church *not* to witness. Another pastor expressed it like this:

> Evangelism never seemed to be an "issue" in the New Testament. That is to say, one does not find the apostles urging, exhorting, scolding, planning, and organizing for evangelistic programs. In the apostolic Church, evangelism was somehow "assumed," and it functioned without special techniques or special programs. Evangelism happened! Issuing effortlessly from the community of the believers as light from the sun, it was automatic, spontaneous, continuous, and contagious.[2]

Those sentiments are idealistic. They are not realistic. The New Testament is replete with commands to witness. There are five passages on the Great Commission. Commands are given to be obeyed, and obedience demands effort.

To Be Evangelistic

Most Christians agree that the spiritual life will affect evangelism. The question is how. For one thing, walking with the Lord produces godliness; and godliness, in turn, affects evangelism.

Lack of godliness can discredit not only your testimony but the reputation of the Word of God. In Titus 2, Paul tells Titus to speak to the aged men, the aged women, the young men, and the young women. Each group should develop godly character. In the midst of that discussion, Paul suggests that if the young women develop this godliness they will prevent the word of God's being blasphemed. In the New Testament, the phrase "word of God"

---

2. Richard Halverson, "Methods of Personal Evangelism," p. 343.

sometimes refers to the gospel. Most commentators interpret it that way in this verse. The gospel ought to make a woman a better wife. If the wife were unruly, her unbelieving husband might blame the gospel. Godliness will prevent that from happening.

On the positive side, godliness will produce a good reputation for you and the gospel. In 1 Thessalonians 4:11–12 Paul exhorts believers to live a calm, peaceful, industrious life, paying attention to their own work so that they may "walk properly toward those who are outside." The word "properly" (*euschēmōn*) literally means "good form," "honestly," "becoming." As one commentator suggests, the idea is "so as to cause no offense." One of the requirements of an elder ("bishop") is that he "have a good testimony among those who are outside" (1 Tim. 3:7). Likewise, a witness must have a good reputation in the world.

A godly life may win a person to Christ. In 1 Peter 3:1 Peter tells believing wives to submit to their disbelieving husbands that they may "without a word" win their husbands by their conduct, which is to be pure, coupled with respect. In 1 Corinthians 7 Paul tells the believing partner not to leave his unbelieving mate. "For," he says in verse 16, "How do you know, O wife, whether you will save your husband? Or how do you know, O husband, whether you will save your wife?"

That does not mean that a godly life guarantees the conversion of an unsaved friend or family member. In 1 Peter 3:1 Peter says "may." The word "won" is in the subjunctive mood, which is the mood of probability. Joseph Lightfoot interprets 1 Corinthians 7:16 to mean that it is a "reasonable chance."[3] The believer may convert the unbeliever, or he may not.

Nor does it mean that the person must see the life of the witness before he hears the message of the witness. The Ethiopian eunuch had not observed Philip's life before he trusted Christ. He had been to Jerusalem and had probably met Christians, but even so, it was a short visit, and it was not someone's life that led him to Christ.

To know the Lord and walk with Him creates a desire for others to know Him. In Romans 10:1 Paul says, "My heart's desire and prayer to God for Israel is that they may be saved." The fruit of the Spirit is love. Love desires the best for someone. Thus, when

---

3. Joseph B. Lightfoot, *Notes on Epistles of St. Paul from Unpublished Commentaries*, p. 227.

you love God and as a result love people, you want to see them saved. George Whitefield prayed, "Oh Lord, give me souls or take my soul." Praying Hyde, a missionary in India, pleaded, "Father, give me these souls or I die."

Walking with the Lord will also produce an effort to see people saved. As love and the desire to see people saved grows, it will break forth and at least attempt to witness. Jesus said, "Come after Me, and I will make you become fishers of men" (Mark 1:17). Notice that He said "fishers," not necessarily "catchers." The degree of success in fishing depends on the skill of the fisherman, the supply of fish in his fishing hole, the bait, and even the time of day. Fishermen fish sometimes with success and sometimes with disappointment. Likewise, followers of Christ may not always catch, but they want to and try to fish.

I once went with a friend of mine to eat in a small, natural-food cafe. The place was popular and always crowded at noon. The procedure was to order your food at the counter and then search for a place to sit. A lady, sitting at a table, saw us standing and said, "You can sit here, if you would like. I'm about to leave." We thanked her and sat down. My friend began to engage her in conversation. In a friendly, warm way, he was being curious and conversational. But as I listened I knew he was trying to steer the conversation toward things spiritual. Before he succeeded, she had to leave and return to work. After her departure, he looked at me and said, "Oh, well. I was at least fishing." He had not even mentioned the Lord, the Bible, or anything about Christianity, but he was fishing or at least preparing to fish. That is what walking with the Lord will do for you: it will make you fish.

The point of this chapter is that there is a great deal of foggy thinking about the spiritual life and about evangelism. For example, some think that if you are spiritual you will automatically, without effort, be evangelistic. Or that being spiritual means you will be successful. Or, worse yet, that by being evangelistic you will be spiritual. The biblical truth is that the spiritual life is a life of faith that demands obedience and effort. Walking with the Lord produces godliness, a desire to see people saved, and even attempts at fishing for men.

In 1888, the chairman of the Keswick Convention wrote a letter to the lay secretary of the Church Missionary Society. In it he said, "A new thought has been given to me. Consecration and the evangelization of the world ought to go together." Amen!

16

Praying People into Heaven

Lewis Sperry Chafer, the founder of Dallas Seminary, once wrote a book entitled *True Evangelism*. The subtitle is a tip-off to his point of view: "Winning Souls by Prayer." In the book he said, "While the believer-priest may intercede on behalf of the fellow-members in the body of Christ, it is the privilege of his co-partnership with Christ to intercede for the lost; and the answer to that prayer will be the going forth of the Spirit to convict them of sin, of righteousness and of judgment."[1]

Numerous stories from church history tell of believers interceding for unbelievers. Every Christian ever involved in evangelism has found himself spontaneously praying for someone's salvation. Although there is much disagreement about many areas of evangelism, surely there must be agreement over this one aspect of witnessing.

But such is not the case. There are questions. Where in the New Testament is a believer instructed to pray for the salvation of a non-Christian? What is to be prayed for? Is prayer for someone's salvation proper in light of the fact that each person must choose? Dr. Earl Radmacher once preached a sermon in which he pointed out that prayer in the New Testament is for believers, not for unbelievers. Is it appropriate, then, to pray for the salvation of

1. Lewis Sperry Chafer, *True Evangelism*, p. 88.

sinners? What is the place of prayer in evangelism? Can we pray people into heaven? Is prayer for a sinner's salvation proper? And what can be biblically prayed for in evangelism?

PRAYER SHOULD PRECEDE EVANGELISM

In the New Testament, prayer is connected with evangelism. The Lord's parting instructions to the seventy are recorded in Luke 10:1-24. In verse 2, He tells them to pray. In verse 3, He tells them to go. Obviously, prayer precedes the going.

Perhaps following that example, the early church prayed before preaching the gospel. In Acts 4:29, they pleaded with the Lord for boldness. In Acts 4:31, they spoke about the Lord with boldness. The pattern is plain. They prayed and then evangelized. Paul taught that prayer preceded evangelism. In Colossians 4:2-4 he requested that the Colossians pray for him. The request, in this case, concerned his evangelistic ministry. The concept is clear: prayer precedes the preaching of the gospel.

Thus, in the gospels, in Acts, and in the epistles, prayer is connected to evangelism. It comes before it, not after it. That is not to say that prayer should not take place during or after evangelism. It is to say that if prayer does not take place until after, it is late.

Perhaps if we prayed more we would win more. In Acts 2 they pray for ten days, Peter preaches for ten minutes, and 3,000 get saved. Today, churches pray for ten minutes, preach for ten days, and three get saved. It is reported that A.C. Dixon once said, "When we rely upon organization, we get what organization can do; when we rely upon education, we get what education can do; when we rely upon eloquence, we get what eloquence can do, and so on. Nor am I disposed to undervalue any of these things in their proper place, but when we rely upon prayer, we get what God can do."

So there is a connection between prayer and evangelism. But for what do we pray?

PRAYING EVANGELISTICALLY

The New Testament indicates that there are a number of things for which we are to pray. For example, it teaches that we are to pray for peace. In 1 Timothy 2:1-2, Paul exhorts the men of the congregation to pray for those in authority that *"we"* may lead a quiet and peaceful life. In verses 3 and 4, he gives the reason for such a habit: "For this is good and acceptable in the sight of God our Savior, who desires all men to be saved." As peace prevails, the gospel spreads. William Hendriksen says, "In more ways than one, conditions of tranquility and calm promote the spread of the gospel of salvation."[2] Though people have been saved during periods of public turmoil and trouble, the gospel, like warm butter, spreads more easily during periods of public peace. During the campus demonstrations of the sixties and seventies, students were not interested in talking about "religion." Their attention was riveted to the war in Viet Nam.

Paul expresses a similar idea in 2 Thessalonians 3:1-2. The Thessalonians are invited to pray that the gospel will have "free course" (*trechō*, literally "run," or "swiftly advance"). They also solicited prayer that Paul, Silas, and Timothy would be delivered from "unreasonable and wicked men." "Unreasonable" (*atopos*) means "out of place," "perverse," "outrageous." "Wicked" (*ponēros*) means "bad," not just in the passive sense, but in the active sense; that is, not being content to corrupt itself, it wants to corrupt others as well. Paul is asking for prayer that they be delivered from unsaved, outrageous Jews who were turning others against them. If this small war ceased and peace prevailed, the gospel would more swiftly advance.

Second, the New Testament indicates that we are to pray for laborers. In Luke 10:2 the Lord says, "The harvest truly is great, but the laborers are few; therefore pray the Lord of the harvest to send out laborers into His harvest." The Lord looks on a harvest-ready field and sees people who are ready to be saved, like a ripe wheat ready for the sickle. But He laments that there is a lack of manpower. So pray that the sovereign Lord of harvests, and heaven, and the whole earth will dispatch a labor force into the great harvest. Believers must pray for God to send laborers into the fields of the world.

In Ephesians 4, Paul teaches that God gives gifts to men and gifted men to the church. One of these gifts is the gift of evangelism. Because of the recent history of the twentieth century, churches

2. William Hendriksen, *A Commentary on I & II Timothy and Titus,* p. 95.

tend to think of an evangelist as an outstanding public figure like Finney, Moody, or Graham. But the evangelist may also be a layman who has a spiritual gift of personal evangelism. Church members should pray that God would grace their church with people who have the gift of evangelism.

Third, we are to pray for opportunity. In Colossians 4:3, Paul desires prayer for himself and that God would open to him and to Timothy a "door of utterance" (KJV*) that they might speak the gospel. Joseph B. Lightfoot translates this verse, "A door of admission for the word, i.e., an opportunity of preaching the gospel."[3]

Imagine Paul and Timothy arriving in a new town where the gospel had never been preached, where they had never been, and where they knew no one. The one thing they needed, and needed badly, was an opportunity, a door of utterance, a place to start. This truth also applies to getting an opportunity, not just in the city, but in the life of an individual. When Paul wrote to the Colossians he was in prison. Perhaps He was asking for an opportunity to effectually present the gospel to another prisoner, or to a guard. Maybe he needed to be put with a certain person, or once with him he needed an opening to present the gospel. At any rate, Paul asked them to pray that he would get opportunity.

Fourth, we are to pray for boldness. In Acts 4:29, the Jerusalem Christians pray to the Lord that they might, with all boldness, speak the word. "Boldness" (*parrēsia*) simply means "plainness of speech." It is not rudeness. It is freedom to speak openly. A burdened believer may have an opportunity and not take it because of fear. So the concerned Christian needs opportunity and boldness.

In Ephesians 6:19, Paul asks the Ephesians to pray for him that he might speak boldly. Imagine that! Paul, the great, mighty, fearless apostle is asking prayer that he might be bold. If Paul needed prayer for boldness, then obviously so do we.

By the way, note that Acts 4 is a group prayer meeting. Ephesians 6 is a request that a group pray for Paul. Although it may be permissible for an individual to pray for boldness for himself, the example of Scripture is to have a group pray with you and for you.

*King James Version.
3. Joseph B. Lightfoot, *St. Paul's Epistles to the Colossians and Philemon*, p. 231.

All this is good and proper, but there is one question yet unanswered. Is it biblical to pray that a person get saved?

It is biblical to pray for a person to get saved. In Romans 10:1 Paul says, "Brethren, my heart's desire and prayer to God for Israel is that they may be saved." It is not just his desire, but his prayer to God. Acts 7:60 is another incident of praying for sinners to be saved. As he is dying, Stephen prays, "Lord, do not charge them with this sin."

Strong Calvinists object to all of this; they fear praying for one who is not elect. Paul had no such fear. In Acts 26:29 his prayer wish for Agrippa is "I would to God that not only you, but also all who hear me today, might become both almost and altogether such as I am, except for these chains." Paul prayed for non-elect people to be saved.

The Scripture does not bother to explain all the details, but these passages are clear about the practice. Lewis Sperry Chafer says,

> The reason for human intercession in the divine plan has not been wholly revealed. The repeated statements of Scripture that it is a necessary link in the chain that carries the divine energy to the impotent souls of men, in addition to its actual achievement as seen in the world, must be the sufficient evidence of the imperative need for the prayer in connection with the purpose of God. Thus in the Scriptures and in experience it is revealed that God has honored man with an exalted place of co-operation and partnership with Himself in His great projects of human transformation.[4]

In summary, the kind of praying connected with evangelism is praying for peace, laborers, opportunity, boldness, and even the sinner's salvation. In short, pray for believers around the sinner, and for the sinner's salvation.

If you know someone you would like to see saved, pray. Notice that the emphasis of the New Testament seems to be on praying for believers around the sinner. Pray for the right conditions, that nothing distract the unbeliever's attention. Pray for someone to give him the message. Pray that someone is given an opportunity and *boldness* to seize it. Then pray that the person gets saved.

One word of warning: prayer is not a shortcut for the lazy and unprepared. It is a resource for the wise and the diligent. Prayer

4. Lewis Sperry Chafer, *True Evangelism*, p. 89.

is not a substitute for a word of witness. You may be the answer to your own prayer. So after you pray, look for an opportunity, and when it comes take it—with all boldness. Pray like the little girl who said, "Never ask God to do something we can do ourselves." She said, "I asked the Lord to stop my brother from trapping birds, and I believe my prayer was answered. I kicked his trap to pieces." Let us pray, and let us proclaim.

17

On Being Wise, Like a Snake

He disgusts us. There he stands, to our embarrassment. His shoes are not shined, his pants are not pressed, his tie, if he has one, is hanging loose around his neck, and he is screaming at the top of his lungs with a hoarse voice. He is the zealous street-preacher. There he is, standing on the street corner, waving his arms, yelling, "Turn or burn! Repent or perish!" If you get him to stop long enough to interview him, he would be delighted to talk to you. He would tell you that he is witnessing to the world. The world, from his vantage point, is not listening, but he is doing his duty and "tellin' 'em."

The consensus of the Christian community is that such efforts are an embarrassment and ineffective. We applaud his zeal, but we are appalled at his lack of finesse. After all, does the New Testament not say, "Walk in wisdom toward those who are outside"? (Col. 4:5). Definitely! Yet many Christians evidently do not know, or they do not understand, the meaning of that concept. Consequently, they offend, not by what they say, but by the way they say it.

WISDOM BEGINS WITH PURE MOTIVES

Paul does not explain the details of walking in wisdom in Colossians 4, but other passages give us insights. For example, when the Lord sent the disciples to Israel He briefed them by saying, "Be wise as serpents and harmless as doves" (Matt. 10:16). Closely connected with wisdom is being harmless. In fact, biblical wisdom begins with being harmless.

akeraios, the word translated "harmless" in Matthew 10:16, means "unmixed" or "pure," hence "guileless." In other words, their motive was to help, not to harm. They were to be as harmless as a dove. Richard Lenski puts it like this: " . . . without admixture, i.e., of base motives such as falseness, cunning, and the like, the type of this quality being the doves who hurt no one."[1] J. A. Alexander says, "*Harmless* is therefore an inadequate and inexact translation, and the true sense given in the margin (*simple*), of the character required is not mere abstinence from injury to others, but that perfect simplicity and purity of motive, without which all the wisdom of the serpent would be unavailing."[2]

James 3 confirms that wisdom begins with pure motives. James 3:13-18 describes two kinds of wisdom: devilish and divine. James says in verse 14 that devilish wisdom is characterized by bitter envying and strife, that is, self-seeking. He goes on to explain in verse 17 that divine wisdom is first pure. In this context that can only mean pure in motive, not having bitter envying and self-seeking. Godly wisdom, then, begins with pure motives.

Be a dove. Men have been injured and killed by elephants, lions, tigers, and even on occasion by some types of birds, but never by a dove. Before a dove would hurt anyone it would fly away. Don't be a donkey and kick; don't be a spider and kill; be a dove.

WISDOM MEANS COMMON SENSE

Jesus said, "Be wise as a serpent." There are several different Greek words translated "wise." *sophia* refers to skill or intelligence. It is wisdom in the primary and absolute sense of the word. *sunesis* is wisdom in the critical sense of the term. But *phronēsis,* the word used here, is "prudence," that is, practical wisdom or common sense. Wisdom begins with pure motives and ends with common sense.

---

1. Richard C.H. Lenski, *The Interpretation of St. Matthew's Gospel,* p. 399.
2. J.A. Alexander, *The Gospel According to Matthew Explained,* p. 290.

William Hendriksen comments,

> Therefore be keen as the serpents, and guileless as the doves. As
> to the first (cf. Luke 16:8), the serpent is viewed as the very embodiment
> of intellectual acumen or shrewdness (Genesis 3:1). The cautiousness
> and wariness of serpents has become proverbial. The keenness here
> recommended as a human quality involves *insight* into the nature
> of one's surroundings, both personal and material, *circumspection*,
> *sanctified common sense, wisdom* to do the right thing at the right
> time and place in the right manner, a serious attempt always to discover
> the best means to achieve the highest goal, an earnest and honest
> search for an answer to such questions as: "How will this word or
> action of mine look in the end?" "How will it affect my own future,
> that of my neighbor, God's glory?" "Is this the best way to handle
> the problem or is there a better way?"[3]

START WHERE THEY ARE

In 1 Corinthians 9, Paul speaks of using common sense by starting
where people are. In verse 20 he says, "And to the Jews I became
as a Jew, that I might win Jews." He acted as they acted. He conformed
to their customs. He did not do this to the point of iniquity, but
he did it to identify with them. For example, he had Timothy
circumcised. Verse 21 says, "To those who are without law, as without
law (not being without law toward God, but under law toward
Christ), that I might win those who are without law." He was willing
to behave as a Gentile when with the Gentiles. He did not insist
on keeping the Jewish observances. He quoted heathen poets and
took as his text an inscription on a heathen altar. Yet he was not
without the moral law before God. He kept himself under the
law of Christ. Paul also applies the principle to believers. To a
weak Christian he became as one who was weak, that he might
gain him. He says, "I have become all things to all men, that I
might by all means save some." Verse 23 adds, "Now this I do
for the gospel's sake."

Let me illustrate. Walt asked his church for a Sunday school class.
The church agreed but told him he would have to go out and
get his own pupils. So Walt began to beat the bushes. He came
across Howie busily playing marbles and asked him to go to Sunday

---

3. William Hendriksen, *New Testament Commentary: An Exposition of the Gospel
   According to Matthew*, p. 461.

school. Howie was not interested in the least in Walt's Sunday school, but quickly agreed when Walt challenged him to a game of marbles. After Howie lost all of his marbles he agreed to go to Sunday school to learn how to get them back. Walt was a warm, simple-minded man who worked in a tool and die shop. He was well over six feet tall with a heart as big as his size 14 shoes. Walt loved the Lord and his class of young boys. One day he took his class on a hike through Fairmont Park in Philadelphia. During the hike he took aside a young man who was having trouble in school and at home and introduced that troubled youth to Jesus Christ. The boy responded by receiving Christ as his Savior. Today, that youngster is affectionately known as "Prof" by students at Dallas Theological Seminary. He is Dr. Howard Hendricks. Walt used wisdom. He started where Howie was.

DON'T QUARREL

"A servant of the Lord must not quarrel but be gentle to all" (2 Tim. 2:24). God's servant is not to quibble or quarrel. He must not be irritable, intolerant, sarcastic, or scornful. Rather, he is to be kind, gentle, and gracious.

Soul-winners are not to attack a sinner like a soldier on a campaign to conquer an opponent. If a haughty and hostile attitude provokes a debate, the believer may win the argument and lose the convert. So don't argue. Many mistakenly view the sinner as a soul that must be overcome and conquered at all costs. If he resists, he is stupid and stubborn and must be persuaded. That attitude can lead to a raised voice, a strained neck, even a clenched fist. Tempers flare.

Don't be caught in that trap. Be a light and shine; don't be lightning and burn. Remember that tact is the knack for making a point without making an enemy.

ARGUE

Paul used wisdom in evangelism; he argued. Acts 17:2 says he "reasoned with them." The Greek word (*dialegomai*) means "to discuss, to argue." Verse 3 says, "Explaining and demonstrating." *paratithēmi*, translated "demonstrating," was employed for quoting evidence. So Paul did argue. He explained and quoted evidence.

Like a lawyer presenting a case, the apostle used logic and reason. Acts 17 says that this was his custom. Paul disputed with the Jews in the synagogue and daily with people in the marketplace. In Acts 24:25 we are told that he reasoned with Felix.

Robert Smith argues that the Christian should argue.

> Jesus never hesitated to argue with people if that was the most effective means of getting at the heart of the matter. As a great teacher, however, he was never interested simply in mental gymnastics, as were medieval schoolmen; his goal was to tear down barriers men erect against God. He not only warded off the attacks of opponents but thrust his point to the heart of his foes, as a fencer jabs with a rapier. He used reproach, fiery indignation, even sarcasm, and so effectively that at times his opponents slinked off with their tails between their legs. They feared to engage him in the mortal combat he handled so well.
>
> Unlike Socrates and Aristotle, who were more concerned about the intellectual search for truth than for the searcher himself, Jesus sought to bring men into the life more abundant. Exposé of fallacies did not suffice. Commitment and discipleship were his goals. He sought always to get at the essence of the questions, sometimes passing by the outward form of them—as with Nicodemus (John 3) or the woman at the well (John 4)—to probe the depths. He knew which points to explore and which to avoid. The cutting edge of his argument peeled away the mish-mash and phony fronts men hide behind so that many could say, "No man ever spake like this man" (John 7:46).[4]

Second Timothy 2:24 exhorts us to never argue. Yet these examples urge us to argue. How are these two seeming opposites to be reconciled?

The answer is to use arguments but never to be argumentative. To argue means to present a thesis and then evidence to support that thesis. The thesis, in this case, may be: (1) Jesus is God in the flesh; (2) Jesus' death fully paid for sin and paves the way for eternal life; (3) salvation is by faith and not by works. The evidence for these arguments come from Scripture, logic, testimony, example, quotations, and so on. Yet while presenting the case, the contender for the faith must not be contentious. The New Testament contains two words for "argue." One, *dialaleō*, suggests

---

4. Robert Smith, "Should the Christian Argue?" p. 15.

"contention and strife." The other, *athleō*, used of Paul's practice, simply means "debating, arguing, mingling thought with thought." Charles Finney, a converted lawyer, won thousands to Christ by arguing like a lawyer for sinners to be converted.

USE CURRENT EVENTS

Luke 13:1 tells of a time when Pilate slaughtered Galileans who were sacrificing. The popular view was that those sufferers had merited their deaths. Erdman says, "The common fallacy was supposing that exceptional suffering is a proof of exceptional guilt on the part of men."[5] Jesus seized the opportunity to teach that temporary exemption is a mark of the grace of God. All are sinners. All deserve judgment. Delayed judgment should be regarded as a merciful opportunity to repent. Jesus emphasized this truth by referring to a recent calamity in which eighteen men had been crushed by the fall of a tower. Their fate was not the sign of their special sinfulness, but a warning to others that they would likewise suffer unless they repented of their sins. The lesson for evangelism today is that, like Jesus, we need to capitalize on current events.

The young lady whom the airline computer had placed beside me on the plane was excited. She was on her way to her wedding and was at thirty thousand feet before the plane left the ground. I listened as she told me how she and her fiancé had met, dated, and decided to get married. When she finally stopped long enough to rest I said, "You know, many people are down on marriage, but not me. I'm happily married to a wonderful woman and have three children. I believe wedlock is wonderful. I think marriage is the second most important decision of your life." Startled, she blurted, "Second? What's first?" By using the current event in her life I was able to suggest that the first, and most important decision of life, was who a person would spend eternity with, and the second was with whom he would spend the rest of his life.

To sum up, wisdom in evangelism is using common sense with pure motives. It is being simple–hearted, without being a simpleton. It is being smart without being a smart aleck.

In commenting on Matthew 10:16, Spurgeon says,

---

5. C.R. Erdman, *The Gospel of Luke, An Exposition*, p. 148.

The disciples were sent to fierce men to convince them, and therefore they must be wise; to convert them, and therefore they must be gentle. The weapons of Christians are that they are weaponless. They are to be prudent, discreet, "wise as serpents"; but they are to be loving, peaceful, "harmless as doves." The Christian missionary will need to be wary, to avoid receiving harm; but he must be of a guileless mind, that he do no harm. We are called to be martyrs, not maniacs; we are to be simple-hearted, but we are not simpletons.[6]

To us who know the Lord, the gospel is a sweet, sweet story; but to a sinner headed for the judgment of God, sin, death, and hell are bitter pills to swallow. Thus we must be wise as we deliver the message.

A small boy was asked how summer camp could be improved. He answered, "Put more sugar in the lemonade." More sugar and less lemon is needed in evangelism. In this case, it is all right to sugar-coat the "gos-pill." I like chocolate-chip ice cream, but when I go fishing I use worms, because fish like worms.

6.   Charles H. Spurgeon, *Spurgeon's Popular Exposition of Matthew*, p. 70.

18

What Made Paul So Bold?

Have you ever feared telling someone about the Lord? You wanted to present the gospel to him, so you pondered it, prayed about it, and planned. When the moment of truth came and you were face to face with the individual—it happened. A hesitation, a reluctance, a fear gripped you. You were like a small boy who had a bit part in a church play. At the appropriate moment he was to bounce out on the stage and say, "It is I. Be not afraid." But when the moment of truth arrived, he appeared on the stage and proclaimed, "It's me, and I'm scared to death!"

To make matters worse, you then met someone who, with no restraint, spoke openly and freely about Jesus Christ. Perhaps it was a new convert who in the excitement and enthusiasm of his new-found faith was telling everyone about Christ. Maybe it was an excitable extrovert who talked all the time anyway and thus did not seem to have any difficulty talking about Christ. I suspect many Christians look longingly at believers with such boldness and wish they had it, too. Then they decide, "That's not me. I'm not outgoing."

How does one become bold? Is it just a matter of personality? Paul was obviously bold. What made him like that? He tells us in 1 Thessalonians 2:1-8.

For you yourselves know, brethren, that our coming to you was not in vain. But even after we had suffered before and were spitefully treated at Philippi, as you know, we were bold in our God to speak to you the gospel of God in much conflict. For our exhortation did not come from deceit or uncleanness, nor was it in guile. But as we have been approved by God to be entrusted with the gospel, even so we speak, not as pleasing men, but God who tests our hearts. For neither at any time did we use flattering words, as you know, nor a cloak for covetousness—God is witness. Nor did we seek glory from men, either from you or from others, when we might have made demands as apostles of Christ. But we were gentle among you, just as a nursing mother cherishes her own children. So, affectionately longing for you, we were well pleased to impart to you not only the gospel of God, but also our own lives, because you had become dear to us.

PAUL WAS BOLD

That is his point in verses 1 and 2. Paul begins by saying that his visit to them was not empty. Their visit was not hollow activity, but rather, he says in verse 2, "we were bold." Boldness is not bluntness. Our English word gives us the impression of aggressive and crass behavior, but the Greek, *parrēsiazomai,* simply means "the freedom to speak."

In November 1977 Sam Blair, a sports writer for the *Dallas Morning News,* said to Tom Landry, legendary coach of the Dallas Cowboys, "You have lapped the league a couple of times, in terms of longevity, and you're not even winded. But in 1960, when you became the Cowboys' coach, did you ever have any idea the job would last this long?" Landry replied, "It's amazing. If I had had as much knowledge as I have now, I would have been more concerned when I moved into this job. Still I think my experience in 1958 when I became a Christian, a person with goals beyond winning and losing football games, gave me a different insight. I wasn't really even concerned about being fired." That is boldness. He was not rude, or blunt, or crass, but he did have the freedom to speak openly about Christ.

Paul was not only bold, he was bold in the face of opposition. He says (v. 2), "We had suffered before and were spitefully treated at Philippi, as you know." The suffering refers to physical beating, and the spiteful treatment refers to being insulted and humiliated. Remember Philippi? Acts 16 tells us they were arrested and beaten with many stripes. Jewish law was forty stripes save one, but this was a Roman scourging. The Roman custom depended upon the caprice of the judge, and it was a brutal ordeal. He was humiliated, arrested on false charges, stripped, publicly beaten without trial, and thrown into prison as a common criminal.

Imagine it. Lift up Pauls' shirt and look at that bare back. See those long, large, red welts. Look at the cuts. You can be sure they hurt for months afterwards. I can just imagine that as Paul and Silas left Philippi, Silas, with his hand on his back, pleaded with Paul, "Let's keep a low profile in the next town; at least until my back heals." But not Paul. He got to Thessalonica, and he spoke out openly and boldly. Sure enough: trouble started all over again. Verse 2 says that he spoke with much contention, that is, struggle. He met opposition again, but even with a bruised back and a shamed spirit, he spoke again. Paul was bold in the face of opposition.

When we get a snicker we shut up. When we are ridiculed we rivet our mouth shut like a locked trunk. Paul got opposition and spoke openly. What made him do that? He explains in this passage. Verse 3 begins with the little word "for." So does verse 5. That is an indication that Paul is giving us the two reasons he spoke so openly about the gospel.

He Was Convinced His Message Was from God

In verses 3 and 4, Paul talks about the origin of his message. In verse 3, he says it did not come from man: "Our exhortation did not come from deceit." The Greek word "deceit" (*planē*) means "error." The ancient Greeks believed Zeus was the god who controlled all weather and decided the outcome of all battles. That was erroneous. So an exhortation to worship Zeus was an exhortation of error. Paul is saying that his preaching did not originate from error.

Paul continues, "or uncleanness." "Uncleanness" (*akatharsia*) here probably refers to sexual impurity. It regularly appears with adultery and fornication. So Paul is saying, "My preaching did not originate from sexual impurity." That may strike us as odd, but the ancient world would have immediately got the point. The Greek temple housed priestesses who served as prostitutes. An exhortation to worship there was an invitation to wallow in uncleanness.

Paul adds, "Nor was it in guile." He is not talking here about origin so much as sphere. "Guile" (*dolos*) means "bait, snare, deceit."

In other words, his preaching was not composed of deceit or trickery. A fisherman uses a worm as bait to deceive and trick a fish. The fish thinks he is getting something to eat and ends up getting eaten. The religions of the ancient world were deceitful. Paul is declaring that his is not.

Paul's point, thus far, is that his exhortation is not of men; it is not of error, uncleanness, nor in deceit. Well, where did it come from? He tells us that in verse 4.

Paul claimed the gospel was of God. He says in verse 4 that God put him in trust and holds him accountable. Therefore he speaks not to please men, but God. In other words, he is saying, "I speak the gospel because it is not from the corruption of men, but it is from the commission of God."

Paul was God's trustee. Let us suppose a wealthy man died and made you the trustee of his estate. His instructions were that you were to give the wealth away to a certain kind of person. So you start looking for that kind of person. When you find him, you have no hesitation or reluctance in saying, "I want to give you this large sum of silver." The person might say, "That's got to be wrong. You must have stolen it. It's hot. What's the trick?" You would respond, "Take this. It's yours. I am not mistaken. It is not out of uncleanness. It is not stolen. There is no trick. I know a wealthy man who died, and he wants you to have this."

That is something of what Paul is saying. He is claiming, "That's why I speak so openly. My exhortation is not a mistake or illegal. There is no deceit. It is simply that God has made me a trustee of the gospel." Paul was convinced that his message was of God, and that made him bold.

But there was a second reason for his boldness.

PAUL WAS CONCERNED ABOUT PEOPLE

In verses 5–8, Paul talks about his motives. At first it may appear that he is talking about his technique, but careful analysis will reveal that he is talking more about motives than methods.

In verses 5 and 6 he tells us what his motive is not. He says that his motive is not to serve himself: "For neither at any time did we use flattering words." The Greek word *kolakeia* was used of flattery that had selfish motives. There is a difference between appreciation and flattery. One is sincere, and the other is insincere;

one is selfless, the other is selfish. He adds, "Nor a cloak for covetousness." He had not used preaching the gospel as a coat to cover his covetousness like a robber uses an overcoat to cover his gun. There was no hidden selfishness in what he had done. He also contends, "Nor did we seek glory from men." He had not selfishly sought recognition and reputation, yet he does add, "We might have made demands as apostles of Christ." As an apostle he did have a right to recognition, but he did not seek it. His point is that his motive is not to serve himself.

In verses 7 and 8, Paul tells us that his motive is to serve others. Verse 7 says, "We were gentle among you, just as a nursing mother cherishes her own children." Because we loved you, we were gentle with you. A mother loves her small infant, so she tenderly, carefully, gently cares for it. In verse 8 he adds, "So, affectionately longing for you . . . you had become dear to us." Paul and Silas were willing to give them their lives as well as the gospel. The point is that Paul loved them, so he served them and not himself.

Wendell Wilkie once asked Franklin Delano Roosevelt, "Mr. President, why do you keep that frail, sickly man, Harry Hopkins, at your elbow?" FDR replied, "Mr. Wilkie, through that door flows an incessant stream of men and women who almost invariably want something from me. Harry Hopkins wants only to serve me. That's why he's near me." People do not care how much you know until they know how much you care.

To sum up, Paul is saying in this passage, "I was bold to speak the gospel to you, even in the face of opposition, because I knew my message was from God, and my motives were to serve you."

Could it be that if we were convinced the message was of God and were committed to serving people, we would speak? If that is the case, then the issue is not personality, it is spirituality. An outspoken person does not speak just because he is outgoing. As a matter of fact, it may be harder for outgoing people to speak, since they want more than anything to be liked. The issue is not personality, it is spirituality. If you are convinced and committed, you will communicate. If you are not, you will not communicate. If you focus on yourself, you will be silent. If you focus on the Lord's command, and you are concerned about others, you will speak.

Hugh Lattimer once preached before King Henry VIII. Henry

was greatly displeased by the boldness in the sermon and ordered Lattimer to preach again on the following Sunday and apologize for the offence he had given. The next Sunday, after reading his text, he thus began his sermon:

> Hugh Lattimer, dost thou know before whom thou are this day to speak? To the high and mighty monarch, the king's most excellent majesty, who can take away thy life, if thou offendest. Therefore, take heed that thou speakest not a word that may displease. But then consider well, Hugh, dost thou not know from whence thou comest— upon Whose message thou are sent? Even by the great and mighty God, Who is all-present and Who beholdeth all thy ways and Who is able to cast thy soul into hell! Therefore, take care that thou deliverest thy message faithfully.

He then preached the same sermon he had preached the preceding Sunday—and with considerably more energy.

Part 5

The Practice of Personal Evangelism

19

Where Do I Start?

Knowing about evangelism, the details of the message, and how to present it is one thing; but knowing practically where to start and how to proceed is another. When confronted with an individual who needs Christ, the issue is how to approach him. There are two basic philosophies of personal evangelism.

Friendship evangelism starts by making friends. By taking time to establish a relationship and winning the friendship you win the right to be heard. Then, and only then, according to this view, do you share the gospel.

On the other end of the spectrum is the view that says, "That's not necessary. Get a method of presenting the gospel and get started. Witness to everyone you can, everyone you meet. Winning friends is great, but you need to win strangers." This view is sometimes called "cold turkey evangelism."

Each side marshals biblical support for its view and wages war on the other view. The friendship folks could well cite Luke 16:1–9. In the parable of the unjust steward, Jesus taught the disciples to use their money and influence to "make friends for yourselves." The ultimate purpose was so that "they may receive you into everlasting habitations." (By the way, this view also goes to John 4 for support, but that passage supports the other side. In John 4 Jesus witnessed to a stranger, not a friend.) The cold turkey persuasion could point to Acts 8. Philip did not take time to establish a relationship or a friendship; he immediately plunged into the issue of salvation.

Problems occur with both views. Some end up witnessing only to friends and use friendship evangelism as an excuse. The Great Commission becomes, "Go into all the world and win friends." On the other hand, the cold turkey extremists insist that *every* person they meet, even those they meet just for a moment, must be spoken to. Such legalism can kick the heart out of evangelism.

Where, oh, where, is the balanced, biblical view? After wrestling with this subject and the related Scripture passages for many years, I have developed a philosophy of personal evangelism. It could be summarized as follows:

ASSUME DIVINE DESIGN

A practical, biblical approach to evangelism begins with an attitude. Every believer ought to assume that the people in his life are not there by accident but by divine design. In Genesis we are told the story of Joseph: motivated by jealousy, his brothers sold him into slavery; Ishmaelites bought him, transported him to Egypt, and sold him into slavery there; Potiphar's wife accused him, and he ended up in prison; eventually, the dreamer arose from prison all the way to the palace. Now, a humanist might conclude that the caravan just happened to come along and just happened to be headed for Egypt , and so on. The humanist would conclude that this poor boy had a lot of bad luck. That was not Joseph's view. He concluded, "You meant evil against me; but God meant it for good, in order to bring it about as it is this day, to save many people alive" (Gen. 50:20). What happened to Joseph was no accident. It was all by divine design. God allowed those people to be in his life for a purpose.

When Paul was in prison at Rome, the Philippians became concerned. They sent financial aid and Epaphroditus to him. Paul's response was the book of Philippians. In chapter 1, verses 12 and 13, Paul explains that what happened to him resulted in the furthering of the gospel. He was chained to guards, so he won them to Christ. Paul didn't believe that he was in jail because of some misfortune or accident. His view was that he had a divine appointment.

Some people hate their circumstances. They feel they are in a prison. The truth is, God has put them there to teach them and to use them. Their attitude needs to change, and until it does they will not have much impact on their surroundings.

BE WARM AND FRIENDLY TO EVERYONE

After adopting a proper biblical attitude, every Christian should then decide to be a warm, friendly, concerned neighbor to everyone. First Peter 3:8 says, "Finally, all of you be of one mind, having compassion for one another; love as brothers, be tenderhearted, be courteous." Believers are to be concerned, compassionate, and courteous. Such conduct is not just for special occasions like witnessing; it is to be the life-style of the saint.

When I meet people, whether on a plane or at a social function, I automatically want to know them. That is done, at first, by asking questions like, "Where are you from, originally?" "What do you do for a living?" "Are you married?" These are three of my favorites. We talk about their family and their job. In other words, we talk about their favorite topic of conversation—themselves.

Now some will say, "That's not me. I'm not outgoing."

My response to that would be, "Since when is your personality so sacred? Change!"

USE GOOD JUDGMENT, BUT PRESENT THE GOSPEL

After you have gotten to know the person, then—unless there is a good reason not to—begin to present the gospel. That is, ask an opening question and start going through a basic outline of what a person needs to do to be saved.

Philip met the Ethiopian and with little or no introduction plowed into a discussion of spiritual things. Thousands and perhaps millions since have done the same thing. Church members taking a religious survey have led their neighbors to Christ on the first visit. Zealous students have led fellow students to Christ in the first conversation. Cold turkey evangelism works.

Yet the better part of wisdom may be to wait. There may be good reasons for not witnessing to a particular person on the first meeting. For example, if you know that you will have more contact with the person, it might be wise to wait. Preaching the gospel to every member of the family the next time you see them after conversion is not a good idea. Family members are probably the most difficult to reach. Jesus said that a prophet is without honor in his own country. You will discover the same with your family, so be tactful, but don't be so tactful that you lose the attack. The same advice applies to your neighbors and your fellow workers. Do not witness to every fellow employee the first day on the job (unless they bring up the subject). But do make plans for getting the gospel to all with whom you work.

If you know the person has been "turned off" by religion, definitely don't jump into evangelism. Pushy parents, over–zealous preachers, and unwise peers have caused some to be turned off, and thus they have turned away from the gospel. They want nothing to do with God, the Bible, the church, or Christianity. They need love, not another lecture.

If you know the person has an intellectual problem, start with this need. If a person does not believe that Jesus is God in the flesh and has intellectual objections to such doctrines, telling him he needs to trust Christ will probably have little impact. In his case, intelligently discuss his problem.

The real point is to begin. Give them the gospel.

Let's face it. We are out to see people change. Too many Christians have soaked up the world's idea that we should live and let live. God told us to preach the gospel so that people will be changed by the power of God. Some Christians are so weak that they are not trying to change others. They are fighting—struggling—to keep *others* from changing *them*.

HOW TO HANDLE INTERRUPTIONS

If you know of no good reason not to, then attempt to present the gospel at every opportunity. You will be surprised at the favorable response. If the person has a problem he will let you know. He will ask a question, or he will object.

If he asks a question that concerns the gospel presentation, answer it. These kinds of questions usually deal with clarification. If the question is an objection outside the issue of the gospel, ask him if it can be dealt with after the presentation. For example, if he blurts out in the middle of the "Roman Road," "Do you believe that Jonah was swallowed by a whale?" respond by saying, "That's a good question. Would you mind if I finish the presentation and answer that afterwards?" I usually write the question on a piece of paper so as not to forget it and to show him that I intend to answer it later; then I finish the gospel presentation. In many cases the person will trust Christ. He may even say afterwards, "Oh, I'm not worried about that question, anyway." If, when you get to the end of the presentation and are asking for a decision to trust Christ, he again brings up a question, then by all means stop and answer it.

Sometimes people ask questions and bring up objections that are not original with them. They have heard someone else bring it up, and it stuck with them. Those are the kinds of interruptions you can successfully temporarily sidetrack. There are, however, questions and objections with which the person has struggled. These have become "hangups." If that is the case, you dare not continue until the objection is dealt with.

MEET HIM WHERE HE IS AND TAKE HIM AS FAR AS YOU CAN GO

When you have determined where he is, meet him at that point and take him as far as you can toward the Lord. It is as if every person you meet is on either side of a line. The line is salvation.

Everyone to the right of the line is a believer. Believers can be subdivided into categories ranging from babes to mature saints. First John 2:12–14 divides Christians into little children, young men, and fathers. Babes are immature, self–centered, and noisy. They need feeding, changing, and lots of attention. Children are immature, self–centered, and active. They need feeding and attention, but they are beginning to learn. Young men are growing and ambitious. They need counsel and direction. Fathers are mature and productive. They meet needs, yet they have needs. They still need feeding and can need encouragement. The members of the Body are to minister to one another. Every believer you meet has spiritual needs, and you need to be a positive ministering influence in his life. As much as he will let you and as much as you are able, you should be taking every believer in your life toward maturity.

Everyone to the left of the line is lost. This crowd can also be divided into categories, and our job is to bring them as far as we can toward salvation. Some are religious. They accept the Bible as the Word of God and Christ as the Son of God. A witness needs to start where they are and take them as far toward salvation as possible. Others are plagued with pressing personal problems and may or may not be religious, but they are hurting. Again, the proper evangelistic approach is to begin where they are and take them as far as we can toward the Lord. That might mean relating to them how Christ has solved some of those same problems in your life. Still others are intellectuals. They do not accept the Savior, the Scriptures, or even the supernatural. They have objections, questions, arguments, and rebuttals. With these, as with others, we must begin where they are and take them as far as we can toward salvation. That may mean suggesting a book for them to read.

In the next several chapters each of these unsaved groups will be discussed in detail. The point here is that we must start where they are and take them as far as we can.

A scriptural and practical approach to personal evangelism assumes that God is working, and it is friendly. So begin where a non-Christian is and take him as far toward the Lord as you can. There may be good reasons for the person's not receiving the Lord, but until that occurs, proceed as if rejection is not going to happen.

The key is to begin. A trip of a thousand miles begins with the first step. If you don't start, you will definitely never finish. For fear of not being able to finish many never start. In the case of evangelism, it is better to fish and catch nothing than not to fish at all.

Off Vancouver Island in the Pacific Ocean there is a stretch of water known as the Zone of Silence. This area is accoustically dead. No sound penetrates it at any time. Because no buoy, bell, or siren can warn ships of dangerous reefs, there have been many shipwrecks in that area, and many a vessel lies ruined on the ocean floor. Are you a zone of silence?

20

How to Lead a Person to Christ

A number of methods have been developed to enable a believer to lead a non-believer to Christ. For many years the "Roman Road" approach was popular. The points of the presentation followed the outline of Romans. A similar system called "Four Things God Wants You to Know" employed the same basic outline, but used different verses. Then Bill Bright of Campus Crusade for Christ introduced the idea of a booklet. No sooner was that concept successful than booklets multiplied like rabbits. In the meantime, a Presbyterian pastor, James Kennedy, created an evangelistic explosion that, like Mount St. Helens, fell all over the United States. Today, there are scores of methods for leading people to Christ.

I have often wondered which method is biblical and best. How did they do it in the New Testament? How did Paul lead someone to Christ? How did Peter? They didn't have a Bible (that is, the New Testament), or a booklet. How did they teach others to do it? What was their method?

Then one day it dawned on me. We do have one clear instance of an evangelist's leading someone to Christ. How did Philip, the evangelist, do it? What method did he use? Let us study this case history, described in Acts 8:26–40, to discern how to lead a person to Christ.

TO COMMENCE, ASK A QUESTION

Philip had just concluded a city-wide evangelistic crusade. He was traveling back to Jerusalem, evangelizing on the way, when he received word that he was to journey south. Once in southern Palestine, he came upon an Ethiopian eunuch. This was no ordinary Ethiopian citizen. He was a man of position and power, in charge of the treasury of Ethiopia. The fact that he was sitting in a chariot indicates that he was a man of high rank. Traveling in a chariot then would be like riding in a Cadillac limousine now. He was also a pious man, for he had been to Jerusalem to worship. That means that he was either a Jew (which is not likely), a proselyte, or a God-fearer. A proselyte was a Gentile who had converted to Judaism. Proselytes were circumcised and kept the law. God-fearers were only loosely connected to Judaism. They attended the synagogues and read the Jewish Scriptures.

This pious political leader was sitting in his chariot reading Isaiah (Acts 8:28). He was reading aloud (*anagnōsis*, the word used here, refers to public reading). Verse 30 indicates that, for Philip "heard" him read. Reading in ancient times was invariably aloud because the words were written together with no space between words, no punctuation, and no capital letters. Deciphering the text was facilitated by reading aloud. So as Philip approached the chariot he heard the Ethiopian reading and simply inquired, "Do you understand what you are reading?" The Ethiopian responded in the negative and invited Philip to aid him. Philip was able to explain the passage in Isaiah, as well as the gospel. Notice that Philip started the evangelistic conversation with a question.

In his first epistle, Peter implies that a question is the way to start an evangelistic discussion. He instructs in 1 Peter 3:15, "But sanctify the Lord God in your hearts, and always be ready to give a defense to everyone who asks you a reason for the hope that is in you, with meekness and fear." In other words, living a sanctified life will provoke questions. On more than one occasion I have led someone to Christ because he saw the godly life of a Christian and started asking questions.

Whether you provoke a question with your life-style or pose a question with your lips, the transition from a secular to a spiritual conversation is the question. The question is the line of demarcation. Once you cross it, it is easier to go ahead than to go back.

Successful methods today open with a question. Campus Crusade asks, "Have you ever heard of the Four Spiritual Laws?" James Kennedy's method recommends two questions: (1) "Have you gotten to the place in your spiritual life where you know for certain that if you were to die today you would go to heaven?" (2) "Suppose that you were to die tonight and stand before God and He were to say to you, 'Why should I let you into My heaven?' What would you say?" Jack Hyles uses "If you died now, do you know that you would go to heaven?" Campus Crusade works with university students, Kennedy attracts professional people, and Hyles labors among the working class. Yet they all use the same basic principle to get an evangelistic conversation going—they ask a question.

If you have not done this before your reaction might be, "That's a bold approach. Won't it offend people?" If you are genuinely concerned about people, and if you are courteous, you will not offend them. I personally have used this method for more than twenty years, and I do not recall ever offending anyone by my approach.

A lady was waiting in a shopping mall for her husband. A Christian approached her, gave her a tract, and asked if she knew for sure she was going to heaven. As they talked, her husband returned, and she had to leave. As they walked away the husband asked, "What did he want?" The wife replied, "He wanted to know if I were going to heaven." The husband responded with "That's none of his business." To which the wife said, "Funny, but if you could have seen the expression on his face you would have thought that it was."

To Communicate, Use the Scripture

What happens after the question is asked? In Philip's case, he used the Scripture to present Christ (v. 32). The New Testament recognizes throughout that faith comes by hearing and hearing by the Word of God. But that is not to say that a Bible must be used, or that a tract, or leaflet, or booklet cannot be used. It is to say that the tract, or whatever, should at least quote the Scripture. Remember Hebrews 4:12. An evangelist is like a mailman: he delivers someone else's message.

Philip used the Scripture and preached Jesus. He didn't expound Genesis 1, he explained Isaiah 53. It was not creation he was communicating, it was Christ. If a person is to be saved, he must hear about Christ (Acts 4:12). Jesus Himself said, "If I am lifted up from the earth, [I] will draw all peoples to Myself" (John 12:32).

Yes, Christ is the heart of the Scriptures,
He is the theme they convey;
So when you would witness to sinners,
Point them to Jesus, the Way.

Philip used the Scripture to preach Christ and His cross. Acts 8:32 says, "The place in the Scripture which he read was this." *periochē*, the word translated "place," literally means a portion, or section. Commentators generally suggest that Philip and the eunuch discussed the whole paragraph. That paragraph in Isaiah 53 deals with the death of Christ.

For that matter, Luke quotes part of the passage. What he quotes clearly proves they talked about Christ's death. The point of Acts 8:32 is that Christ died like a lamb, submissively and silently. In verse 33 Philip goes on to describe the suffering of an innocent and unresisting victim. The phrase "in His humiliation His justice was taken away" means that in His death, justice was withheld. The fair trial due Him was not given Him. "Who will declare His generation?" is difficult to interpret. The Hebrew text and context seems to support the idea that this means "He will set forth the wickedness of His contemporaries." The next sentence of verse 33 is the proof and demonstration of their sin: "For His life is taken from the earth." Clearly this passage describes Christ's death. Thus, Philip used the Scripture to present Christ and His cross.

In leading a person to Christ, the cross must be presented. It is the heart of the gospel (1 Cor. 15:3-4). Paul boldly proclaims, "For I determined not to know anything among you except Jesus Christ and Him crucified" (1 Cor. 2:2). The cross is the power of God to salvation (1 Cor. 1:18; Rom. 1:16).

TO CLOSE, STRESS FAITH

After Christ and His death for sin have been presented, the need for faith needs to be stressed. After Philip's sermon based on Isaiah 53, they continued journeying southward. This time, they traveled together. When they came to a water hole the eunuch volunteered, "See, here is water. What hinders me from being baptized?" (Acts 8:36). He could have heard about baptism at Jerusalem, but more than likely he heard about it from Philip. The evangelist indicated that there was one basic requirement for baptism—faith. That is in contrast to Judaism. In Judaism two things kept him out: being a Gentile and being a eunuch. But all that is necessary for salvation is faith in Christ. The treasurer testified of his trust in the Savior, and Philip baptized him.

Philip closed this transaction by stressing faith. There are two objections to that observation. (1) The conversation took place after the discussion of Isaiah 53, and the context was baptism, not salvation. How do we know that Philip stressed faith at the close of the original conversation? (2) The passage is not in some Greek manuscripts. How do we know this happened at all?

There may be a problem with concluding from this passage that faith ought to be stressed at the close. But there is no question that throughout Acts and the New Testament that is the issue. In Acts 10, Peter preached to Cornelius and his household. He used the Scriptures. He preached Christ, especially the gospel, and he stressed faith (10:43). In Acts 16, the Philippian jailer heard Paul and Silas praying and singing praises. He undoubtedly heard then about Christ, the cross, and conversion. When he asked, "What must I do to be saved?" Paul emphasized—believe! (Acts 16:30–31). These men stressed faith and made clear that the persons needed to trust Christ.

The biblical principles of presenting the gospel are: (1) open with a question; (2) use Scripture to present Christ crucified; and (3) close with the issue of faith.

It is really simple, but most Christians feel inadequate. They will look at Acts 8 and think, *but Philip was an evangelist, and I'm not Billy Graham. I could never do that.* It is true that Philip is called an evangelist, but that is not until Acts 21:8. Throughout this passage he is just Philip. As a matter of fact, at this point he was not an evangelist but a deacon (Acts 6:1–5), which simply means a servant.

If you want to know what it takes, note what he did. In Acts 8:27, he "went." In verse 30, he "said." Verse 35 says he "opened his mouth." And in verse 37, he "said" again. If you can go, open your mouth, ask a question, speak, and make a statement, you can lead a person to Christ.

We think that because we are not biblical men we cannot do what they did. For example, we look at Moses, who spoke before Pharaoh and worked miracles, led a million distraught Jews out of Egypt and parted the Red Sea—but we forget that Moses felt inadequate. When first called, his objection was "I can't speak." Maybe that is the requirement; for when we are weak, He is strong.

21

How I Do It

For several years I taught evangelism at Dallas Theological Seminary. Every year I gave a lecture on the biblical principles of leading a person to Christ. From Acts 8, I explained that Philip, the deacon turned evangelist, opened with a question, presented Christ from the Scriptures, and closed by emphasizing faith. Every year the same thing happened. A student would raise his hand and ask, "But how do *you* do it?" So every year I had to explain how I did it.

That is what I would like to do for you. I would like to share with you how I present the gospel to a non-Christian. Before I do, I would like to make several preliminary observations.

This method is not inspired. I am not suggesting in any way that my method is the best or the only way to go. God has not chiseled it in a stone or given it to me in a vision.

I am not even claiming originality. My method is basically the "Roman Road." I do not know who composed the Roman Road, or where it was born, but I do know that it has been used by thousands of Christians for many years.

This method works. I have used the Roman Road in one form or another for over twenty years. I have used it as a teenager, a young adult, a middle-aged man. I have used it successfully on the East and West coasts, in the Midwest, the North, and the South. I have seen the Lord bring many people to Himself with this simple presentation of the gospel.

This method can be imitated easily. You can copy this method. Copyright in this case means the right to copy, and you can do it with ease.

The first thing I do is establish rapport. In a warm, friendly, tactful way, I try to find out as much as possible about the person, as I would if I met someone at a party. I ask such things as where he is from and what he does for a living. I usually ask about his family: for instance, how many children and how old. Obviously, not all these questions apply to all the people I talk to. The point is, I spend time getting to know the person. This also gives him a chance to get to know me. I want him to feel comfortable and relaxed.

For me, the transition from talking about secular things to discussing spiritual things is a question. I personally use three questions: (1) Do you know for sure you are going to heaven? The response is usually, "No, I am not sure," or, "I hope so." (2) Then I ask, Has anyone ever taken a Bible and shown you how you can know for sure you are going to heaven? That question almost always gets a negative reply. (3) So I ask, May I? That inquiry too almost always gets a positive reply. Please note carefully that if a person should say no, which for me is extremely rare, I do not, contrary to the advice of some soul winners, proceed. In my opinion, to insist on preaching the gospel to an unwilling hearer is unbiblical, unwise, and unethical.

If you have not done this before, you might think these questions are frontal and offensive. My observation is that when Christians are courteous and genuinely concerned, people are not offended but really desire to talk about spiritual things. So at this point I take out my Bible and usually a piece of paper and a pen. Turning to Romans 3:23 I say, "In order to know you are going to heaven you need to understand several things."

ALL HAVE SINNED (ROM. 3:23)

I read Romans 3:23 and point out that it says *all* have sinned. The first thing I do is say, "That includes me. I have sinned." That is important. When talking to a person about spiritual things, whether it is intended or not, he sometimes feels you consider yourself to be better than he is. Maybe it is because the whole assumption of this conversation is, I am going to heaven and you are not. After all, I am showing you how to get there. Most people feel that goodness gets you to heaven and badness keeps you out. So without verbalizing it, he may feel that you think you are somehow superior. In order to avoid that pitfall, I begin by saying, "That includes me. I have sinned."

Then I ask, "*If* I were to ask you *if* you were a sinner, what would you say?" That is as diplomatically as that question can be asked.

By the way, this is a conversation, not a sermon. It is a dialogue, not a monologue. I want the other person to talk to me as well.

At any rate, most people readily admit that they have sinned, especially in the nonthreatening context of my admission that I have too. I usually say, "Right. This verse says all have sinned. That obviously includes both of us."

Next I ask, "What would you say sin is? We have both agreed we are sinners, now let's define sin." As you can imagine, I have received a variety of answers. The most common include "I am not perfect," or, "I have made some mistakes." I then move the conversation from speculation to Scripture by asking , "What do you think the Bible means by sin?" The person will often bring God in, if he hasn't before. I point out that the Bible says that sin is breaking God's law (1 John 3:4).

Then I get specific. I do not list all of the Ten Commandments, but I at least bring up one, and usually several. With children, or even teenagers, I often ask, "Have you ever disobeyed your parents? With adults, I use the ninth commandment: "Have you ever told a lie?" Everyone will admit that at some time in his life he has lied. So I point out that that is what sin is. It is breaking God's law. One example is that we have lied.

I do not get too specific. I do not ask, "Have you ever committed adultery?" unless I know for sure the person has, and he knows that I know.

My transition to the next point is as follows: "We have both admitted to each other that we have broken God's law. Any time you break a law there is a penalty. If you run a stop sign, the penalty is a fine. If you rob a filling station, the penalty is jail. What is the penalty for breaking God's law?"

THE PENALTY OF SIN IS DEATH (ROM. 6:23a)

Pointing to Romans 6:23 I read out loud, "The wages of sin is death." The wages of work is money, but the wages of sin is death.

In other words, what I earn—the penalty, the punishment of sin—is death. Death is separation.

The Bible speaks of two kinds of death, that is, two kinds of separation. The first is physical death, which is separation of the body and the soul. If I were to die right now my body would fall to the floor, but my soul, the real me, would go somewhere else. But the Bible speaks of another death, one it calls the second death. This second death is separation of the soul from God. Now, the penalty of sin is death, spiritual death, separation from God. To put it simply—hell.

My transition to the next point is: "All this is bad news, but there is good news."

CHRIST DIED IN OUR PLACE TO PAY FOR OUR SIN (ROM. 5:8)

I then read Romans 5:8 to the person. "God demonstrates His own love toward us, in that while we were still sinners, Christ died for us." At this point I ask, "What is the penalty of sin?" "Death" is usually the answer. "Right. Now, what did Christ do?" He answers, "Christ died." Again, "Right. Now, put these two things together. The penalty of sin is death, but Christ died for us. That means He died in our place to pay for what we did. Frankly, this means that since Christ died, I do not have to pay.

"Let me illustrate. Suppose a ten-year-old boy were standing here. Let's also suppose that this boy had disobeyed his father, and his father said, 'When you get home tonight you're going to get a spanking.' Then imagine I went home with the boy and said to the father, 'Let me take the spanking for the little boy.' I know this may sound a bit wild, but let's suppose the father agreed. I took the boy's spanking. If that happened, would the boy get the spanking? The obvious answer is no. I took his place and paid his penalty. Now that is what this is all about. I have sinned. The penalty is death, but Christ died for us. The boy disobeyed his father. The penalty was a spanking, but I got it instead of the boy. You see, because Christ died and paid for sin, we do not have to go to hell."

After giving the illustration, I emphasize the truth by using three fingers to review. Holding up three fingers and pointing to the first I say, "I have sinned." Pointing to the second I repeat, "The penalty of sin is death." Indicating the third finger I emphasize, "Christ died for my sins." The finger approach may sound like something you would use with children; I do. I also use it with adults, educated adults.

Someone asked Bill Bright once, "Do you use the Four Spiritual Laws with college professors?" He replied, "Yes, and I read the booklet more slowly."

I cannot emphasize enough that the death of Jesus Christ is the issue. It must be carefully presented. The Spirit of God will use the preaching of the cross to enlighten and save.

On more than one occasion I have literally seen the spiritual "lights" come on at this point in the presentation. The person says, "Wow. You mean Christ died and that settles it?" I have seen the Holy Spirit take over in such a way that I didn't have to finish. Overwhelmed by the truth of Christ's death, the person trusted Christ before I could tell him he needed to do just that. I would like to say that all, or most, conversions are like that, but that is not true.

So I go to the fourth and final point. My transition to it is to simply say, " There is one thing God asks of you."

FAITH IN CHRIST SAVES FROM SIN (EPH. 2:8-9)

Finding Ephesians 2:8-9, I read aloud, "For by grace you have been saved through faith, and that not of yourselves; it is the gift of God, not of works, lest anyone should boast." I then explain that a person must have faith in Christ in order to be saved from sin. Works we do for God cannot save from sin, because works do not pay the penalty for sin. It is not what I do for God that saves, it is what God has done for me.

I then explain that faith, in the New Testament, consists of two elements. The first element of biblical faith is accepting something as true. In the case of faith in Christ it is believing: (1) that Christ is the Son of God; (2) that Christ died for sin; and (3) that Christ arose from the dead. I then simply ask the person if he believes these things are true. The second element in biblical faith is trusting something or someone. In the case of faith in Christ, a person must trust Christ, that is, depend on Christ plus nothing for the forgiveness of sins.

I say to the person, "Let me make this clear. We are saved by faith, that is, by trusting Jesus Christ in His death on the cross to get us to heaven. It is not just believing facts about Christ; it is trusting on Christ to get you to heaven."

I then illustrate the concept of faith. Finding a chair I say, "I could stand beside this chair and say, 'I believe it will hold me up. I believe it has four legs, a bottom, and a back.' But it is not holding me up." I then sit on the chair and say, "Now I'm trusting it. I not only believe the facts about it, but I'm depending on it to keep me off the floor. It is one thing to say I believe the chair will hold me up. It is another to trust the chair to hold me up. Biblical faith is sitting on the chair."

After illustrating the concept of faith I invite the person to trust Christ by simply asking, "Would you like to trust Christ right now? That is, would you like to tell God that you are willing to depend on Christ plus nothing to get you to heaven?"

If the person says, "Yes," I then say to him, "All right, let's pray together. This is what we'll say. 'God, I admit that I have sinned. I believe Jesus Christ died for my sin, and I want to trust Him to save me right now.' Before you pray that, I want you to understand that saying the prayer does not save you. Trusting Christ does. So, when you say this I want you to say it to God, and remember that this means that you are telling Him that as of now you are going to trust in Christ to get you to heaven, plus nothing else. OK, bow your head and pray with me."

I then repeat the prayer, sentence by sentence, and have him repeat it after me. As soon as we have finished praying I look at the person and ask, "If you were to die right now, where would you go?" If the person has really understood he will say, "Heaven." I then respond by asking, "Why should God let you into heaven?" I expect him to tell me, "Because Christ died to pay for my sin."

I then explain, "When a person trusts Christ, the Bible says he knows Christ. And yet, it also teaches that we are then to get to know Him better and better. It's like meeting a person. You know him, but not very well. You know Christ, but now you need to get to know Him intimately. That is done by communication. You talk to Him and He talks to you. Spiritually, that is Bible reading and prayer. I suggest you start reading the book of Philippians. Read one chapter a day for thirty days. Then choose another book. (For a more detailed discussion on follow-up, see chap. 25.)

CONCLUSION

As you can see, my way of leading someone to Christ follows the theological outline of Romans and covers all of the points of the message demanded by the Great Commission. But the real issue is this: you need a method of leading someone to Christ. The command of Christ is that the gospel be preached to every creature. The very nature of that task necessitates that every Christian be involved. If you are to carry out your responsibility, you must have a practical way of presenting the penetrating facts of salvation.

That is not to say that you must adopt my method; it is only to say that you need to get a method. All I ask is that your method be biblical and clear. Nor is it to say that you will never vary from even your own method. You will. I do—frequently. But if you have no method, you will probably not witness at all; and if you do, you will more than likely do a poor job. If you have a method, you will present the gospel more often and better. Furthermore, when you do depart from it, you will know why and what you are doing.

So, if you do not have a method that is biblical and clear, start with the Roman Road. If you want a booklet, I suggest *How to Have a Happy and Meaningful Life.* It can be obtained from Dallas Theological Seminary, 3909 Swiss Avenue, Dallas, Texas 75204. Other good methods are available. The point is to start with a method. Change it if you wish, modify it if you must, but start with a method.

A lady once told an evangelist, "I don't like your method." He replied, "I'm not totally satisfied with it myself. What's yours?" She answered, "I don't have one," to which the evangelist responded, "I like my method better than yours."

22

The Religious Lost

There are at least three kinds of lost people in America: the religious, the plagued, and the intellectual. If you introduce the subject of salvation in a conversation, a religious person will start telling about his religion. Then there is a growing group in America who, when you bring up salvation, will want to discuss a pressing personal problem; I call these "the plagued." And of course, there are intellectuals who, when the Bible comes up, will raise objections.

These three types appear on the pages of Scripture. As a matter of fact, they appear in the gospels during the life of Christ. It is fascinating to watch the way Christ dealt with them. He did not use the same exact approach in each case.

In this chapter we will discuss the religious lost.

Did you ever talk to someone about the Lord and have him tell you how religious he is? What do you do then? Did you ever witness and have the person inform you that he felt one had to work his way to heaven by being good? How do you respond to that? Or, did you ever present the gospel only to have a person say, "I believe all of that," even though you knew he was not saved? How do you handle that?

I recall witnessing once to an elderly lady. Her response to me was: "As soon as my son-in-law gets out of the service he's going into the ministry." Many times when I have asked people about their relationship to Jesus Christ, they have responded by talking about the next closest thing to Him that is close to them. Perhaps that is part of being blind. The problem is how to deal with the religious lost. Jesus teaches us by example in John 3.

MANY ARE RELIGIOUS – BUT LOST

Nicodemus was a religious man. John 3:1 says he was a Pharisee. The very word today has negative connotations, and, granted, there were some negative aspects, but it was not all negative. For one thing, the Pharisees believed the Old Testament. The Sadducees did not. The Pharisees believed in the existence of angels and the resurrection of the dead. The Sadducees denied both doctrines. The Pharisees were religious conservatives. The Sadducees were liberal. Furthermore, the Pharisees were zealous. They not only had points to ponder in their heads, they had passion in their hearts. Their zeal was for the law. So eager were they to keep the law of Moses that they added law upon law upon law. That is where they got into trouble. They had so many little laws that they could not possibly keep them all. They tripped over themselves in the process of trying. Thus, they became hypocrites. Nicodemus, being a Pharisee, accepted many of the presuppositions that Jesus did. He also readily admitted that Jesus was from God.

People like this exist today. They are not hypocrites but religious people who accept all our presuppositions—and yet are lost. Actually, there are more of these people in the United States than we realize. For many years the Gallup Poll has surveyed the religious beliefs of people in America. One of the things discovered is that most people in the United States accept our presuppositions. That is, they believe there is a God, that the Bible is inspired, and that Jesus is the Son of God. They may not understand the details, or even what all that means, but they have a good, healthy attitude toward God and the Bible. It may have some mistakes in it, according to them, but the Bible is the "Good Book." Mind you, the Gallup Poll has discovered that the *majority* of Americans believe all of that.

RELIGIOUS PEOPLE NEED TO BE CONFRONTED WITH THE GOSPEL

Nicodemus came asking about spiritual things, and Jesus, with almost no introduction, told him, "Unless one is born of water and the Spirit, he cannot enter the kingdom of God" (John 3:5). Jesus confronted this religious man with spiritual truth immediately. To fully appreciate that, flip the page and compare John 3 with John 4. In John 4 Jesus did not immediately confront the woman at the well. He slowly, tactfully, diplomatically, and yet effectively presented her with some spiritual issues. The reason is that she was an altogether different case. (More of that in the next chapter.) The principle here is to confront the religious person with the gospel. Clearly and simply present a religious man with the gospel of the grace of God. That is what Jesus did. At the end of His conversation, He told Nicodemus that no man has ascended to heaven, but the Son of Man had come to die, and only believers would have eternal life. In a similar fashion, we need a clear and simple presentation of the gospel, and we need to use it on the religious lost.

We have the idea that religious people already know, but they don't. Their church has not told them, their pastor has not preached it; they have not heard it. So with a religious person, take a Bible and clearly spell it all out to him.

A simple presentation of the gospel may do it, but it may not. In the years I've done this I have discovered two issues that often come up and need to be dealt with. One is "works." It is amazing: of all people, religious people ought to know better, but they don't. Many think works are necessary for heaven. When that issue arises I do one of two things. I either use Ephesians 2:8–10 or John 3:16.

Ephesians 2:9 says, "Not *of* works." Verse 10 goes on to say, "We are His workmanship... *for* good works." I point that out and then draw a circle on a piece of paper. I write in the circle "baptism" and say, "If I were to stop people at random on the street and ask, 'What must I do to be saved?' and they said, 'Be baptized,' would they be saved?" The person will usually say, "No." I draw another circle and put in it "church membership." Again I ask if that will get a person to heaven. The person will again say "No." I repeat the process, adding "right living," "good works," and "Jesus Christ plus good works" (sometimes I draw all these circles at once and ask, "Which one are you standing in?"). Then I draw a circle and put "Jesus Christ plus nothing" in it. This technique has helped me to communicate that salvation is by faith and not by works.

I have also used John 3:16. I read it to them as written, and then I quote it to them as their view would revise it. That is, "God so loved the world that He gave His only begotten Son, that whoever believes in Him and gets baptized, and does good works, and lives right, and gives money to the church, should not perish but have everlasting life." The sarcasm communicates.

The other snag is very often the concept of faith. As we have seen in the chapter on faith, the Greek word contains two ideas: believe and trust. A person must both believe the facts about Christ and depend on Christ in order to be saved. The problem is that we say, "Believe on the Lord Jesus Christ and you will be saved" (Acts 16:31), and Americans think that to believe they only need to believe the facts.

At this point, illustrations are indispensable. I have already mentioned the illustration of the chair. It is one thing to believe the chair will hold you up, but it is another to sit in it. The same truth can be illustrated with a car, an airplane, or an elevator. I like to use the airplane when illustrating that it is all Christ and none of you. Getting to heaven is like getting to Japan from Los Angeles. You can't make it on your own. You must depend on an airplane. I like to use the elevator to illustrate that it is Christ plus nothing else. In order to get to the top of a tall building you must put both feet on the elevator. You cannot put one foot on the elevator and one foot on the first floor.

The point of this chapter is simple: confront the religious person with the gospel. The problem with the religious lost man is that he is religious; and because he is religious, he sees no need. He is indifferent. It is easy for us to become indifferent to his indifference. We become unconcerned because he is unconcerned. Or, we are indignant because he does not believe the right things. He doesn't understand. Discussion degenerates into debate, and then we blow our whistle. When my son was four and my daughter was two, they tried to summon birds in our back yard by blowing a whistle. As odd as it sounds, some try to attract others by making noise.

We will never attract anyone by blowing our own whistle. Rather, we must see the need and simply confront the issue. Some people look at a lost religious person and see a barrier and a problem. Others see the possibility of winning someone to Jesus Christ.

23

The Plagued American

For years I criss-crossed the United States as an evangelist. I preached from Connecticut to California, from St. Paul to St. Pete. During those years I became a student of non-Christians. One of the things I discovered was that not all sinners are exactly alike. The more I observed and studied, the more I became convinced that lost people can be grouped. I also discovered that Jesus encountered different types of unbelievers and did not use the same approach with everyone. As a result of examining the American scene and expounding the Scriptures, I have come to the conclusion that there are at least three different, distinct kinds of unsaved people in this country: the religious lost, whom we looked at in the last chapter, the plagued, and the intellectuals.

The plagued American is one who, when you bring up salvation, will bring up a pressing personal problem. The conversation between Christ and the woman at the well illustrates this person and the procedure to be followed.

A GROWING GROUP ARE PLAGUED

Jesus left Judea and headed for Galilee. Instead of taking the normal route of crossing the Jordan River, traveling north, and then recrossing the Jordan into Galilee, He went straight north. Such a course was direct and shorter, but the Jews did not go that way because it was through Samaria; and the Jews hated the Samaritans. As Jesus and the disciples journeyed across Samaria, they came to Sychar. Being weary from the journey, our Lord rested at Jacob's well while the disciples went into the city for food.

While Christ was resting and waiting, a Samaritan woman came to the well to draw water. He asked her for a drink, which ultimately led to a discussion of salvation. Once the subject came up, all kinds of personal issues came out. The woman had several personal problems.

For one thing, she was a Samaritan. The Samaritans were racially mixed. When Assyria conquered the Northern Kingdom, many of the Jews were exported, and many foreigners were imported. The Jews who stayed and the Gentiles who came intermarried. The offspring were half-breeds called Samaritans. The Jews hated them and would have nothing to do with them.

She was also divorced. As a matter of fact, she was not only divorced, but she had been divorced five times and was now living with a man who was not her husband. Divorce is one of the most devastating experiences of life. A person can bury his mate, grieve for a time, and then go on. With divorce, there are scars. Even the innocent party has scars. He or she feels rejected, hurt, forsaken, guilty, and bitter.

The woman at the well was a social outcast. She came to the well at noon and alone. Normally the women came later and together. Because of her divorces and her living with a man who was not her husband, she was alienated. She probably didn't have a female friend. She was probably the subject of jokes and gossip. They laughed behind her back and maybe to her face. She felt unloved, hated, rejected. She no doubt hated herself.

There is a growing group in America who are plagued with pressing personal problems. They are usually more concerned with their immediate personal problems than with the ultimate and permanent issue of salvation. In this group are individuals who feel unloved, rejected, and alienated. There is the fellow whose father did not accept him, or neglected him. Or he could never please his father, no matter how hard he tried. There is the girl with a broken romance or marriage. In this group are also people who are bitter. Because of their treatment at home, they become bitter and carry that bitterness into their adult life.

Often the bitterness is directed toward the church, the preacher, or religious people. An over-zealous religious parent, preacher, or peer has tried to cram religion down his throat. Or, he has been hurt or deceived by a religious person. The guilty are also in this circle. They have sinned, and they know it. They feel guilty because of their sin and are plagued by it.

When my brother was in seminary, he worked in an office that had several secretaries. One day he got into a conversation that naturally turned toward spiritual things. Feeling it was the right time he asked, "Do you know for sure you are going to heaven?" The secretary responded, "Oh, I'm divorced." That is the kind of response you will often get from a plagued person. You bring up salvation, and he will bring up a pressing personal problem. How should you respond?

CULTIVATE THE PLAGUED WITH LOVE

When Jesus encountered a religious person He confronted him with the gospel. When He met a plagued person He cultivated her with love. That is not to say He did not love Nicodemus, or that He did not give the gospel to the woman at the well. It is to say that His primary approach for the Pharisee was *confrontation*, and with the plagued woman it was *cultivation*.

Cultivation includes several things. First, we must *listen*. In John 3, Jesus did most of the talking. In John 4, He listened. In John 3, only three verses record what Nicodemus said, and what he said was usually a question. In John 4, nine verses cover what the Samaritan woman said. God both speaks and listens (Ps. 116:1-2). As the plagued person begins to open up, ask questions about him and his problem. Then listen. Ask more questions. Then listen some more. Ask still more questions, and listen again. Listen, and listen, and listen. This is difficult for a Christian who is sitting on an arsenal of answers, but it is necessary. Howard Hendricks said, "If a person is really hurting, you aren't going to get through to him by sheer enthusiasm. When I encounter a person in this condition, I give him a chance to talk. It shows I'm interested in him as a person, and I may get a chance to really help."[1]

After you listen you will have to speak. What you say first may determine what they hear—or even if they hear. Rather than

---

1. Howard G. Hendricks, *Say It with Love,* pp. 50-51.

immediately diagnosing the disease and prescribing a remedy, you must *identify* with him. When I meet a plagued person I talk with him until he says to me, "You understand me." Needless to say that is easier said than done. How do you do it? The answer is you tell him about the same thing or something similar happening to you. For example, I have talked to many plagued individuals who were suffering from a low self-image. In those cases, I tell him in detail about myself when I was a teenager. I had a great inferiority complex. The key here is "in detail." When he hears me out he knows that I know how he feels.

The problem with this is that he may be telling you something with which you cannot identify. There is nothing in your background like it. What do you do then? The answer is you tell him about the same thing or something similar that has happened to someone you know. I have never been a widow, but I have known a few. By listening to them and watching them, I have been able to understand a little of what their experience is like. On a few occasions I have talked to widows and told them about the experiences of other widows I have known. They then knew that I was aware of at least a bit of what they were going through.

But what if you have never known anyone with a similar experience? Then tell the plagued person about the same thing or something similar happening to someone, even if it is only someone you have read about. Jesus told parables to communicate spiritual truths, but those parables also helped people to identify with Him. Jesus never ran away from home, and He never lived in a pigpen. Yet He told the story of the prodigal son; and every prodigal who has ever heard it has identified with it. One of the highest compliments I was ever paid came from a highly intelligent, highly educated lady with whom I was counseling. After we had talked for some time she said, "You understand. You understand not only the facts, but my feelings." When the person with whom you are talking senses that, you have identified with him.

After you have listened and identified with him, you must *communicate that you love him.* If you have listened well and identified properly, you have already done that to some degree, but more needs to be done. Be patient. First Corinthians 13 describes love. Of all the characteristics of love that are listed, most are negative: Love is not this or that. Of the few positive attributes of love, patience heads the list. Patience is a great part of love.

To communicate to someone that you love him you must be patient.

When someone has a problem, he does not want to talk about it. When he first starts talking about it, he will be slow in getting it out. He may stammer. He may struggle. He may even sit in silence for a moment. Paul urges us to be patient toward all men.

The other thing you can do to communicate your love is to spend time with the individual. For some reason that I am not sure I understand, spending time with someone communicates your care and concern like nothing else you can do. Perhaps it is because when you are unloved, no one has time for you. Or, maybe it is because the essence of love is giving, and taking time is the essence of giving of yourself. This much I do know: it works.

I once led a college student to Christ in Minnesota. She had some theological problems that I had to deal with, and I took the time to do it. Several years later she called me to ask about witnessing to someone she knew at work. The person was a cultist, and frankly I was concerned that she not get confused. I also knew enough of that particular cult to know that it would be very difficult, if not impossible, for her to win her friend to Christ. So I gave her the information she asked for and then added some advice. I simply said, "Don't waste a lot of time with this person." The college student snapped back, "If you had not spent time with me, I'd never be where I am today." She was right. Love, patience, and time can do what arguments, evidence, logic, and persuasion can never do.

Tell them that you are concerned and you care. When it comes to communicating love, there is no substitute for words. Tell them you love them. There is a difference between loving and being in love. I am not talking about romance; I am talking about New Testament love. Tell them that you care. After all, it is biblical (e.g., 1 Thess. 2:8).

Cultivating people with love includes giving them the gospel. Be tactful, but don't lose the offense. True love levels with them. James says, "Be swift to hear, slow to speak" (James 1:19), but do speak. They need your listening ear and your loving heart, but these things will not solve the problem. They need Jesus Christ, so make sure you tell them about Him.

Actually, the gospel speaks to plagued people. To those plagued with sin, Jesus is the Savior. To those unloved ones, Christ is the world's greatest lover. To the broken hearted, He is the healer.

To the rejected, He is the friend who sticks closer than a brother. To the lonely, He is the one who never leaves nor forsakes. Tell them about Him and how He relates to their problem.

The point of this chapter is simple. Cultivate the plagued with love. Listen to them, love them, and level with them. In short, make personal evangelism personal. Give the gospel, but also give yourself.

Not everyone needs this approach. There are some who accept biblical presuppositions and who are prepared; the Nicodemuses and the Ethiopians of the world need only a simple presentation of the gospel. But not all the harvest is white and ready for harvesting. The plagued of this world need cultivation. They need the Lord and His forgiveness, but someone will have to earn the right to be heard before they will hear. The psychologically hungry hear only the growl in their emotional stomachs. That growl drowns out the gospel. Feed the hungry, and he will hear. Love the lonely, and he will listen. Be all things to all men that you might, by all means, win some.

One other word. If there is any group that needs this, it is the "turned off." Some have been "shafted," stabbed in the back, by a so-called Christian. These turned-off ones will be won only by love—love expressed and exercised over a long period of time.

Someone has said, "Every man is an island, and we must row around him to know where to land." In some cases, a port has been prepared, and the Good Ship Salvation can dock without any trouble. In other cases, walls have been built, and the gate will open only to a friend.

24

The Intellectual Wolf

When Jesus sent out the twelve, and again when He sent the seventy, He warned, "I send you out as sheep in the midst of wolves" (Matt. 10:16). The disciples, like lambs, would be defenseless. Wolves, who are vicious and destructive, would attack. Every ambassador of Christ feels that way—defenseless, facing a destructive foe. The wolves Jesus had in mind were religious animals. When the disciples witnessed, the religious wolves growled, showed their teeth, and attacked. These wolves exist today.

But in America, we sheep are not as afraid of the religious wolf as we are the intellectual wolf. We fear that when we speak for Christ some intellectual wolf will rear his head, show his teeth, and pounce on us. Oh, how we fear him. We feel defenseless, convinced that with his superior knowledge or logic he will tear us apart. Imagine trying to convince a Ph.D. in philosophy that there is a God, or a Ph.D. in history that the Bible is inspired! Or persuading a scientist that man did not evolve. How do you reason with an angry student who claims that God is unfair for condemning those who have never heard the gospel? Those are the intellectual wolves.

You may never have witnessed to a Ph.D., but if you witness much, you will meet someone who has been influenced by an intellectual. What do you do? How does a defenseless lamb handle a destructive wolf?

SOME UNBELIEVERS HAVE INTELLECTUAL OBJECTIONS

Jesus encountered those who had intellectual questions and objections. Some were deliberately and maliciously attempting to trap Him. Others were simply not yet convinced. Perhaps the attitude of the intellectual is best expressed by Thomas. Though he was probably a believer at the time, his attitude in John 20 was exactly the same as many intellectuals.

Jesus had been crucified and resurrected. He had appeared to some of the believers, but not yet to Thomas. When told about the resurrection, Thomas said, "Unless I see in His hands the print of the nails, and put my finger into the print of the nails, and put my hand into His side, I will not believe" (John 20:25). Thomas had heard the entire resurrection story with all of its details from Mary Magdelene, Simon Peter, and the other disciples. Thomas listened unmoved and unconvinced. The unanimous testimony of all those people, whose character he knew so well, amounted to nothing. He insisted, "I must see for myself, or I will not believe."

This type of person exists today. When you bring up Christianity he will bring up an intellectual problem. These people either do not accept our presuppositions, or they have an intellectual problem with some facet of Christianity. They are usually well-educated or well-read. University students fall into this category, but frankly not all students are intellectuals, nor will all of them bring up intellectual objections. Some students go to college to get an education, but some go for sports, or for a good time, or to get a good job, or to get a husband. Although any university student may ask an intellectual question, not all will.

CONVINCE THE INTELLECTUAL WITH EVIDENCE

When Jesus appeared again, He dealt with Thomas. He did not condemn him for his unbelief. He did not say Thomas should not have asked questions like that. Rather, He gave him evidence. John 20:27 says that He said to Thomas, "Reach your finger here, and look at My hands; and reach your hand here, and put it into My side. Do not be unbelieving, but believing." Jesus began with his objection and gave him evidence.

Peter taught the same thing in principle. In 1 Peter 3:15 he instructs us to "sanctify the Lord God in your hearts, and always be ready to give a defense to everyone who asks you a reason for the hope that is in you, with meekness and fear." Give a reason for the hope. The principle is to give a reasonable answer to the stated objection.

Let me illustrate. One intellectual objection to Christianity is, "Where did Cain get his wife?" The answer, of course, is that he married his sister. But I go beyond that to show the reasonablenesss of that answer. I admit that there are two problems with it. The first problem is that we know Adam had sons, Cain, Abel, and Seth, but we cannot name any of his daughters. Now, if Adam did not have any daughters, how could Cain marry his sister? The answer to that difficulty is that Adam did have daughters. Genesis 5:4 says so.

But that brings up a second problem. Today, we cannot marry a sister because if a brother marries his sister the mathematical possibilities of the weakness of their line's coming up in their children is very great. The only way to solve that problem is to have perfect parents. That, of course, is exactly the case with Cain and his sister. If the biblical account is accurate at all, Adam and Eve were created by God. Cain and his sister had perfect heredity. There was no prohibition against marrying a near kin then because there was no need for it. Later, when weaknesses developed in the human race, the prohibition against marrying a near kin was established to protect the offspring.

The point is that there is a reasonable answer to the question "Where did Cain get his wife?" and you need to give it to those who ask this question.

This kind of approach creates a problem. Some conclude they can never witness because they will not be able to come up with all those intellectual answers. Some might even be tempted to compile a huge list of possible questions in order to get ready. Before you do either of these things, consider the following.

YOU CAN HANDLE THE QUESTION

Non-Christians usually do not ask the questions Christians ask. We believers hear the Bible and theology discussed and debated. After a while we get the impression that there are a thousand theological, technically tough questions, and some non-Christian is going to dump two hundred of them on us the next time we witness. That is not the case. Granted, there may be many biblical and theological questions, but we forget that most non-Christians are biblical illiterates. They do not ask the questions we do—or the ones we think they do.

Paul Little worked with university students and on university campuses for years. Once, at a Christian college, a number of Christian students wanted him to conduct a mock bull session like the ones he had in fraternity houses on secular campuses. The Christians assumed that they were the fraternity men and that he had come to speak. He gave them one of his presentations and let them ask questions. After the experiment Little said, "I think it's rather significant that they asked all kinds of questions that I'd never been asked in my fifteen years of visiting secular campuses."[1]

Well, if that is the case, what do non-Christians ask? Most non-Christians ask very basic questions, and there are only a few. Paul Little lists seven: What about the heathen? Is Christ the only way to God? Why do the innocent suffer? How can miracles be possible? Isn't the Bible full of errors? Isn't Christian experience psychological? Won't a good moral life get me to heaven?[2]

Don't worry about these questions. Witness! If one comes up, and you can answer it, do so. If you can't, tell them you can't. One of the best pieces of advice a theologian ever gave me was "If you don't know, say you don't know."

When someone asks you a question you don't know—go find the answer. Ask your pastor. Read a book. There are answers. Find them and write the answers in a notebook so you will have them next time.

Therefore, when someone gives you an intellectual objection to Christianity, always begin by giving a reasonable answer to the stated objection. It has been my experience that some people who bring up intellectual objections have honest intellectual questions. They want answers. These people will usually accept good answers, or at least they will accept the reasonableness of the answer.

MORAL ISSUES BEHIND THE QUESTIONS

There are others, however, who will not accept reasonable

1. Paul Little, *How to Give Away Your Faith*, pp. 66-7.
2. Ibid., pp. 67-79.

answers. These people tend to argue. When that happens, the issue is not intellectual, it is moral. So go after the moral issue. As Paul says in 1 Corinthians 14:25, "And thus the secrets of his heart are revealed." In such cases I have observed three moral issues.

One such issue is *guilt*. I was once conducting a rap session with high school teenagers. I told them that they could ask me any question on any subject, and I would try and answer it. Their questions were typical of ones I had received in similar sessions scores of times before. As the session drew to a close, one girl toward the back, who had not said anything, raised her hand. I nodded, and she said, "The Bible says God loves everybody. Then it says that God sends people to hell. How can a loving God do that?" I gave her my answer, and she came back to me with arguments. I answered her arguments, and she answered my answers. The conversation quickly degenerated into an argument. I did not convince her, nor did she convince me. After a few more questions I dismissed the session.

After the session I approached her and said, "I owe you an apology. I really should not have allowed our discussion to become so argumentative." Then I asked, "May I share something with you?" She said, "Yes." So I took her through a basic presentation of the gospel. When I got to Romans 3:23 and suggested that all of us were sinners she began to cry. It was then that this high school senior admitted she had been having an affair with a married man. The one thing she needed was forgiveness. When I finished the presentation of the gospel, she trusted Christ. The reason she did not believe in hell was because she was going there. In her heart she knew she had sinned. Her conscience condemned her, but rather than face the fact of her guilt, she simply denied any future judgment or future hell.

When a person objects to Christianity and does not accept the reasonableness of a reasonable answer, his problem is moral, not intellectual. If the moral problem is guilt, the person will often respond to a simple presentation of the gospel. I have, on these occasions, entered into the intellectual discussion. Then, after the intellectual debate, I have asked, "May I just present something to you?" I have found that just giving them the gospel will sometimes do what all of the intellectual arguments will not do—break down the barriers.

A second moral issue I have discovered is *bitterness*. Many people have been turned off by Christians or Christianity. They have had Christianity crammed down their throats, or they have been stabbed in the back by a Christian. Their response was bitterness. I once witnessed to a fellow who had all kinds of intellectual objections. He was steeped in philosophy and eastern religions. He hurled all kinds of questions at me. I answered them one by one, but then discovered that he would not accept the reasonableness of my answers. So finally I said to him, "Steve, it is my experience when someone resists the reasonableness of Christianity it is because they have been wounded and they are hurting." That got his attention. He looked at me and asked, "What do you mean?" I responded by suggesting that I could be wrong in his case, but that it had been my observation over the years that people who would not accept the reasonableness of Christianity were either guilty or bitter. That opened him up. He then shared with me his bitterness toward his father, who for years pressured him into going to church.

I was not able to lead Steve to Christ, but I was able to present the gospel to him, whereas before he had argued with every sentence. He at least listened and said he would give it serious consideration.

There are still others who are not guilty or bitter; they are just sinful. The moral issue is their own stubborn, *sinful self-will.* When I encounter this type of person I say something like this: "Isn't it possible that what I am telling you is really true, and you've just refused to accept it for the simple reason that you do not want to bow to anyone, not even God?" I have even suggested on these occasions that the person at least needs to be honest with the facts. I then tell them of a student I spoke to once who said to me, "I can't answer your presentation, but it is reasonable. It's just that I refuse to accept it." I then tell the person that if that is the case, I will honor his right to refuse to accept it, but the least he can do is admit that Christianity is reasonable.

In witnessing to intellectuals, there are two extremes we must avoid: anti-intellectualism and intellectualism. Anti-intellectualism is the attitude that says, "Don't bother me with intellectual questions." Don't get sidetracked with people's problems, it says; just preach the simple gospel. The result of such an approach is that the thinking non-Christian will conclude that his honest questions have no answers. Intellectualism says that answers will win the person. To us the answers may be so persuasive that we are convinced they will persuade anyone. We then fall into the trap of relying on the answers. But the gospel is the power of God to salvation. Unless the Holy Spirit works, all our work will be fruitless.

John R. Stott struck the balance when he said, "We cannot pander to man's intellectual arrogance, but we must cater to his intellectual integrity." We must attempt to show the intellectual reasonableness of Christianity by giving him reasonable answers and communicating the gospel clearly.

There is only one way to God—the gospel. But there are many ways to the gospel. The route may be direct, as with the religious person, or it may be indirect. The road may be straight, or it may contain curves. You have to travel the road the person is on when you find him. Just make sure that no matter where you find him, or how many roads he takes, or how many rest stops he insists on, you guide him gently toward the gospel of Jesus Christ.

25

Biblical Follow-Up

There are as many ways to follow up a new convert as there are denominations and para-church organizations. Every successful evangelist develops a new approach that is usually a rehearsal of an old method. One system takes the new babe in Christ through ten steps to maturity, as if the babe will be an adult by the time he finishes the ten lessons. A more modest approach puts all the information in one small booklet and admits that it contains only the first steps for the newborn believer. If reading is too much work, tapes are available. A genuinely new concept combines a booklet and tapes.

What material should be covered in follow-up? Must a method always begin with the assurance of salvation? That certainly seems logical, but is it scriptural? Is that how the apostles started? What method should be employed: booklets, books, or a bag full of tapes?

FOLLOW-THROUGH

Before we follow up, we should follow through. Follow-through is what is done in the initial conversation after a person trusts Christ. Follow-up comes later, once we are sure the person has trusted the Lord.

Follow-through consists of discussing five things. The first is assurance. After I have prayed with a person I usually ask, "If you were to die right now, where would you go?" I want him to tell me, "Heaven." Notice I ask this question before I go to 1 John 5:13, or any other verse on assurance. I want to know what is going on in his mind. Frankly, 1 John 5:13 has been used to trick people into thinking that they have assurance when they really don't. If the person tells me, "Heaven," then I ask, "Why should God let you into His heaven?" The answer I am after is either "Christ died for my sins" or "I have trusted Christ." Once I am convinced that he understands, only then do I show him 1 John 5:13. I use the verse to teach that he can know he is saved.

After discussing assurance, I talk about "getting to know Him." I explain that when a person trusts Christ, the Bible says he knows Christ. And yet it also teaches that we are to get to know Him better and better. It is like a person you have just met: you know him, but not well. Likewise, a Christian knows Christ; but now he needs to get to know Him intimately. That is done by communication. You talk to Him, and He talks to you. Spiritually, that is Bible reading and prayer. I suggest a new convert start with the book of Philippians, reading one chapter a day. When he is finished I suggest that he read through it again and continue the process for the first month of his Christian life. After each day's reading he should pray, thanking God for the blessings and asking Him to meet his current needs.

Follow-through also includes telling a new Christian to be baptized. I explain to him that it is not necessary for salvation. It is only a symbol. A wedding band is not essential for marriage. It is only a symbol of unending love. I also urge him to get it done as soon as possible.

The fourth item in follow-through is telling him about church. I suggest he find a Bible-teaching church to attend, where he can learn the Word of God and grow.

The fifth and final part of follow-through is to ask if the new Christian has any questions. New converts will either have none or will ask something very elementary.

Follow-through is vital. These are the first impressions on the newborn babe's mind. In golf, proper follow-through is absolutely essential for the ball to go straight. Follow-through will launch the new believer in the right direction. But after follow-through comes follow-up. I believe the biblical concept of follow-up is given to us in Acts 2:37–42.

BAPTISM

Follow-up consists of five activities. In Acts 2 Peter preaches and three thousand are saved. Verses 41–42 of that chapter tell us what happened next. First, these new converts were baptized. Thus, baptism is part and parcel of follow-up.

When Jesus gave the Great Commission, He taught that we were to win people to Christ, baptize them, and teach them the Word of God. The instructions are clear. The orders are simple. Yet, many zealous saints and soul-winners do not follow those instructions. Baptism is where they become disobedient. There are two common errors.

Some Christians do not baptize at all. Para-church organizations are consistently disobedient at this point. Their excuse is that they are not a church, and they do not want to become a church, so they skip baptism. But if anyone is going to do what Jesus Christ commanded, he must baptize or at least tell the person the Bible says to get baptized.

The second common error is to reverse the order, putting teaching before baptism. In Matthew 28, and throughout Acts, instruction follows baptism. It does not precede it. Missionaries are particularly guilty of committing this error. Their excuse is that they must wait and see if the decision was real. Evidently that was not the attitude of the apostles.

The truth of the matter is that baptism in New Testament times was done as soon after conversion as possible. In Acts 8 it was performed in the desert. In Acts 9 it was accomplished as soon as someone could be found to do it. In Acts 10 it was done immediately. In Acts 16 it was executed after midnight. There is no evidence at all that anyone in the New Testament waited for any period of time—ever.

INSTRUCTION

Acts 2:42 indicates that after baptism "they continued steadfastly in the apostles' doctrine." *proskartereō*, the word translated "continued steadfastly," literally means "to adhere to." They not only adhered to a system of belief, but they followed the instruction of the twelve.

Notice that it was the apostles' doctrine. The Jews were accustomed to listening to and learning from the rabbis' doctrine.

It could be said that they continued steadfastly in the rabbis' doctrine. The early Christians continued in the *apostles'* doctrine, meaning of course that they listened and learned from the apostles.

The question is, What was the apostles' doctrine? What did they teach? The answer is that eventually the apostles' doctrine took written shape in the New Testament. The apostles' doctrine, then, is the New Testament, especially the epistles. Matthew, Peter, Paul, John, and Jude were apostles who wrote down their teaching. Tradition says that Mark wrote what Peter preached. Luke was the traveling companion of Paul. Thus, apostolic doctrine is the New Testament, and a practical division of New Testament teaching would be: (1) God, including all the members of the Trinity; (2) the Bible; (3) man, including sin, salvation, and sanctification; (4) the family; (5) the church; and (6) the world, including Satan, government, and your job.[1]

FELLOWSHIP

The third part of follow-up is fellowship. Acts 2:42 says, "They continued steadfastly in...fellowship." The Greek word for "fellowship" is *koinonia.* The basic idea of the word is to "share, have in common." The sharing could be sharing things physical (Acts 2:44–45; Phil. 1:5), or it could be socializing. The context here seems to indicate a religious fellowship the disciples had with each other. This much is certain: fellowship involves relationships with people. Part and parcel of follow-up and spiritual growth is having relationships with other believers.

The early Christians did not just learn the apostles' doctrine like a student in a classroom. They became members of a family and developed relationships with each other. Follow-up cannot be done through books or booklets alone. There must be personal fellowship with other believers. Follow-up is not just dispensing information, it is developing individuals. That demands fellowship.

This may just be the most important factor in follow-up and spiritual growth. The precepts and principles from the Word are important, but the personal relationship may be the key to a young

---

1. I have written a small booklet outlining these doctrines and designed to be used in follow-up. It is entitled "Outline for Discipling," and is available from the Church of the Open Door, 550 South Hope Street, Los Angeles, CA 90071.

Christian's getting these concepts. The material and content is important; the apostles' doctrine ought to be taught; but, frankly, regardless of the material used and the subjects covered, relationships are more important (assuming that at least some portion of God's Word is taught). The babe responds to the person feeding as well as to the food being fed. The babe needs someone to care enough to listen as well as to lecture. Cold facts on a page, no matter how accurate, cannot take the place of a personal relationship.

I have taken believers through various kinds of material on numerous occasions. There is no doubt in my mind that when the individual listens to the lecture, I am not really discipling him. But when he begins to ask questions, he begins to learn. When he begins to open up and disclose problems to me, he begins to grow. Time and time again I have taught a person personally, and *after* the lesson he started sharing his hurts. Then he began to interact with spiritual truth and grow. That is why fellowship is such a vital part of follow-up. No book, tape, or even church service can take the place of fellowship.

BREAKING OF BREAD

The fourth part of the Acts 2 follow-up is the breaking of bread. A few interpret this to mean that these believers ate ordinary meals together in their homes. Indeed, the term *breaking of bread* was used, even in the New Testament, of eating an everyday meal (for example, Luke 24:35). The common opinion, however, is that in this passage the phrase "breaking of bread" refers to either the love feast before the Lord's Supper, the Lord's Supper, or both.

The early church observed the Lord's Supper differently than most churches today. They had it every Sunday evening (Acts 20:7). They began with a "potluck" meal, which was called a love feast (Jude 12). Then they concluded the meal by taking bread and wine and remembering the body and blood of our Lord. In Corinth, the love feast was abused.

The rich were gorging themselves and getting drunk, and the poor were going hungry. That is the problem Paul speaks to in 1 Corinthians 11. Several hundred years later, because of such abuses, the love feast was forbidden by the Council of Laodicea (AD 320). Other councils concurred, and gradually it fell into disuse. Thus, today, there is nothing resembling the love feast in most churches.

Be that as it may, the New Testament clearly teaches that believers are to observe the Lord's table. Teaching a new convert to regularly attend the observance of the Lord's table is part of follow-up.

PRAYERS

The fifth and final factor in biblical follow-up is prayers. The first believers were Jews. As Jews they observed regular group prayer meetings. After they became Christians, they still attended those Jewish prayer meetings (see Acts 3:1), yet they evidently began their own appointed seasons of united prayer within the new community. Acts 2:42 refers to those prayer meetings. It was not closed, private prayer; it was community, public prayer. In the Greek text there is an aritcle (*tais*) before "prayers." Richard Rackham, one of the classic commentators on Acts, suggests that this implies regular hours of prayers.[2]

Babes need to learn to talk to the Father. They need to learn to praise, confess, ask, and intercede. Like many other skills, prayer is learned by doing. Nothing encourages a new Christian more than to see God answer prayer. It lets him see that the Lord is alive and loose in the world. The Lord seems particularly pleased to manifest Himself to a babe in Christ by answering his prayers. At the same time, the babe needs to experience the No of an all-wise Father.

WHAT ABOUT THE LOCAL CHURCH?

If all of these elements are included in follow-up, the observation will be that biblical follow-up is a New Testament local church. What Acts 2 demands cannot be done apart from a local church. Churches, not para-church organizations, baptize and observe the Lord's Supper. The moment an organization starts baptizing and observing the Lord's table it becomes, in effect, a local church. God's program for this age is the church. God's plan for maturing believers is a local church. Biblical follow-up is a New Testament local church.

God's illustration of the church is a family. In 1 Corinthians 4:15,

2. Richard B. Rackham, *The Acts of the Apostles,* p. 41.

Paul calls himself a father. In 1 Thessalonians 2, he refers to himself as a mother. He called those whom he won to Christ his own children on several occasions. He called Timothy and Titus his sons in the faith. All these believers were brothers and sisters. For natural growth and normal development a child needs a father, a mother, a family—an extended family. As a machine cannot rear a child physically, neither can books and tapes rear a child spiritually. As friends cannot rear a child like a family, neither can a parachurch group rear a spiritual child like a church. Biblical follow-up is a local church.

Bibliography

Alexander, J.A. *Commentary on the Gospel of Mark.* Grand Rapids: Zondervan, 1864.

———. *The Gospel According to Matthew Explained.* London: James Nisbet, 1861. Reprint. Lynchburg, Va.: James Family Christian Publishers.

Alford, Dean Henry. *The Greek New Testament,* vol. 1. Chicago: Moody, 1968.

Arndt, W.F., and F.W. Gingrich. *A Greek-English Lexicon of the New Testament and Other Early Christian Literature.* Chicago: Chicago U., 1957.

Arnold, Jack. "Principles of Evangelism in the Book of Acts." Master's Thesis, Dallas Theological Seminary, 1961.

Barnhouse, Donald G. *God's River,* vol. 4. Grand Rapids: Eerdmans, 1958.

Bergon, John. *The Last Twelve Verses of Mark.* Grand Rapids: Associated Publishers and Authors, n.d.

Berkhoff, L. *Systematic Theology.* Grand Rapids: Eerdmans, 1941.

Bruce, F.F. *The Acts of the Apostles.* Grand Rapids: Eerdmans, 1965.

Calvin, John. *Institutes of the Christian Religion.* Grand Rapids: Associated Publishers and Authors, n.d.

Chafer, Lewis Sperry. *Systematic Theology,* vols. 3 and 7. Dallas: Dallas Theological Sem., 1948.

True Evangelism. Findlay, Ohio: Dunham, 1919.

Dodd, Charles H. *The Apostolic Preaching and Its Development.* Chicago: Willet, 1937.

Dodds, Marcus. "The Gospel of John." *The Expositor's Greek Testament,* vol. 1, pt. 2, Edited by W.R. Nicoll. Grand Rapids: Eerdmans, n.d.

Erdman, C.R. *The Gospel of Luke, An Explanation.* Philadelphia: Westminster, 1975.

Evans, William. *Great Doctrines of the Bible.* Chicago: Moody, 1949.

Godet, F.L. *Commentary on the Gospel of John,* vol. 1. Reprint. Grand Rapids: Zondervan Publishing House, 1893.

Graham, Billy. "Why Lausanne?" *Christianity Today,* 13 Sept. 1974, p. 4.

Halverson, Richard. "Methods of Personal Evangelism." *One Race, One Gospel, One Task,* vol. 2. World Congress on Evangelism, Berlin, 1966. Minneapolis: World Wide, 1967.

Hendricks, Howard G. *Say It with Love.* Wheaton: Victor, 1973.

Hendricksen, William. *A Commentary on I & II Timothy and Titus.* London: Banner of Truth, 1964.

_____. *New Testament Commentary: An Exposition of the Gospel According to Matthew.* Grand Rapids: Baker, 1973.

Hodge, Charles. *Commentary on the Epistle to the Romans.* Grand Rapids: Eerdmans, 1976.

Knight, Walter B. *Knight's Treasury of Illustrations.* Grand Rapids: Eerdmans, 1963.

_____. *Master Book of Illustrations.* Grand Rapids: Eerdmans, 1956.

"Lausanne Covenant." *Christianity Today,* 16 Aug. 1974, pp. 22-23.

Lenski, Richard C.H. *The Interpretation of the Acts of the Apostles.* Minneapolis: Augsburg, 1961.

_____. *The Interpretation of Luke's Gospel.* Minneapolis: Augsburg, 1961.

_____. *The Interpretation of St. Matthew's Gospel.* Minneapolis: Augsburg, 1961.

Lightfoot, Joseph B. *Notes on Epistles of St. Paul from Unpublished Commentaries.* London: MacMillan, 1895.

_____. *St. Paul's Epistles to the Colossians and Philemon.* Lynn, Mass.: Hendrickson, 1981.

Lindsell, Harold. "Nairobi: Crisis and Credibility." *Christianity Today,* 2 Jan. 1976, pp. 11-12.

Little, Paul. *How to Give Away Your Faith.* Chicago: Inter-Varsity, 1966.

Machen, J. Gresham. *What Is Faith?* Grand Rapids: Eerdmans, 1965.

Mantey, Julius R. "Repentance and Conversion." In *Basic Christian Doctrines,* edited by Carl F.H. Henry. New York: Holt, Rinehart and Winston, 1962.

Morgan, G. Campbell. *Evangelism.* East Northfield, Mass.: The Bookstore, 1904.

Moule, C.F.D. *An Idiom Book of New Testament Greek.* Cambridge: Cambridge U., 1971.

Murdoch, Elmer H. "Step Up to Life." Harrisburg, Pa.: Bethany Fellowship, 1971.

Packer, James I. *Evangelism and the Sovereignty of God.* Chicago: Inter-Varsity, 1961.

Peters, George W. *A Biblical Theology of Missions.* Chicago: Moody, 1972.

Plummer, Alfred. *A Critical and Exegetical Commentary on the Gospel According to Luke.* New York: Scribner's, 1903.

_____. *An Exegetical Commentary on the Gospel According to S. Matthew.* Minneapolis: James Family Christian Publishers, n.d.

The Gospel According to St. John. Cambridge: Cambridge U., 1902.

Post, Roger. "The Meanings of the Words Translated 'Repent' and

'Repentance' in the New Testament." Master's thesis, Wheaton College, 1972.

Rackham, Richard B. *The Acts of the Apostles.* London: Methuen, 1957.

Robertson, A.T. *Word Pictures in the New Testament,* vol. 5. Nashville: Broadman, 1932.

Ryrie, Charles C. *Balancing the Christian Life.* Chicago: Moody, 1969.

The Ryrie Study Bible. King James Version. Chicago: Moody, 1978.

Scofield Reference Bible. London: Oxford U., 1945.

Shedd, William G.T. *A Critical and Doctrinal Commentary on the Epistle of St. Paul to the Romans.* Reprint. Minneapolis: Klock and Klock, 1978.

Shuller, R.P. "The Way." *Sword of the Lord,* 5 Mar. 1971, p. 1.

Smith, Robert. "Should the Christian Argue?" *Christianity Today,* 15 Feb. 1974.

Spurgeon, Charles H. *The Early Years.* Rev. ed. London: Banner of Truth, 1962.

_____. "Faith and Repentance Inseparable." *Metropolitan Tabernacle Pulpit,* vol. 8, Pasadena, Tex.: Pilgrim, 1978.

_____. *Spurgeon's Popular Exposition of Matthew.* Grand Rapids: Zondervan, 1962.

Stott, John R. "The Great Commission." In *One Race, One Gospel, One Task,* vol. 1. World Congress on Evangelism, Berlin, 1966. Minneapolis: World Wide, 1967.

Tan, Paul Lee. *Encyclopedia of 7,700 Illustrations.* Rockville, Md.: Assurance, 1979.

Torrey, Reuben A. *What the Bible Teaches.* New York: Revell, 1898.

Trench, Richard C. *Synonyms of the New Testament.* Grand Rapids: Eerdmans, 1963.

Wagner, C. Peter. "What Is Evangelism?" *Christ the Liberator, Urbana 70.* Downers Grove, Ill.: Inter-Varsity, 1971.

Walvoord, John F. *The Holy Spirit.* Findlay, Ohio: Dunham, 1958.

_____. *The Holy Spirit at Work Today.* Chicago: Moody, 1973.

Westcott, B.F. *The Epistle to the Hebrews.* Grand Rapids: Eerdmans, 1965.

Westcott, B.F. *The Gospel According to John.* London: James Clarke, 1958.

Moody Press, a ministry of the Moody Bible Institute, is designed for education, evangelization, and edification. If we may assist you in knowing more about Christ and the Christian life, please write us without obligation: Moody Press, c/o MLM, Chicago, Illinois 60610.